1. The Popes and Slavery

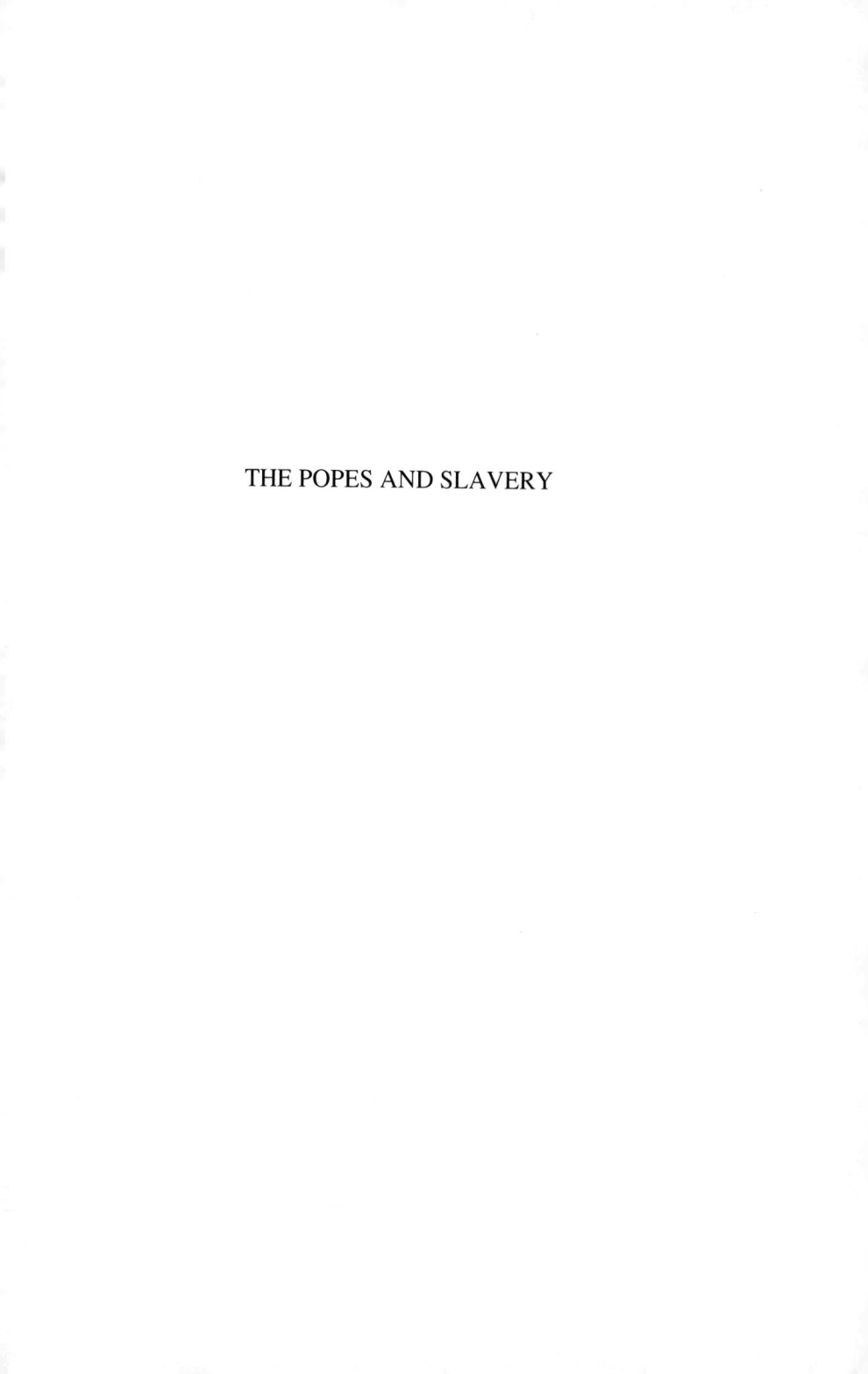

THE POPES AND SLAVERY

THE POPES
and SLAVERY

REV. JOEL S. PANZER

ALBA·HOUSE   NEW·YORK

SOCIETY OF ST. PAUL, 2187 VICTORY BLVD., STATEN ISLAND, NEW YORK 10314

Library of Congress Cataloging-in-Publication Data

Panzer, Joel S.
   The popes and slavery / Joel S. Panzer.
      p.   cm.
   Includes bibliographical references.
   ISBN 0-8189-0764-9
   1. Slavery and the church — Catholic Church — History. 2.Popes —
History. I. Title
HT917.C3P35   1996
261.8'34567 — dc20   96-22753
                                          CIP

Nihil Obstat:
Reverend M. James Divis
Censor Librorum

Imprimatur:
The Most Reverend Fabian W. Bruskewitz, DD, STD
Bishop of Lincoln

The Nihil Obstat and Imprimatur are official declarations
that a book or pamphlet is free of doctrinal or moral error. No
implication is contained therein that those who have granted the
Nihil Obstat and the Imprimatur agree with the contents,
opinions or statements expressed.

Produced and designed in the United States of America by the
Fathers and Brothers of the Society of St. Paul,
2187 Victory Boulevard, Staten Island, New York 10314,
as part of their communications apostolate.

ISBN: 0-8189-0764-9

© Copyright 1996 by the Society of St. Paul

Printing Information:

Current Printing - first digit	1	2	3	4	5	6	7	8	9	10

Year of Current Printing - first year shown

1996	1997	1998	1999	2000	2001	2002

Table of Contents

Foreword vii
Preface ix
Chapter One: THE STATE OF THE QUESTION 1
Chapter Two: PAPAL TEACHINGS ON SLAVERY 7
   The First Hundred Years (1435-1536) 7
      Eugene IV 7
      Alexander VI 11
   The Second Hundred Years (1537-1638) 15
      Paul III 16
      Gregory XIV 29
   The Third Hundred Years (1639-1740) 31
      Urban VIII 31
      Innocent XI 34
   The Last One Hundred and Fifty Years (1741-1890) 38
      Benedict XIV 38
      Gregory XVI 44
      Pius IX 48
      Leo XIII 56
Chapter Three: CONCLUSION 63
Appendix A: Chronology 73
Appendix B: Documents of the Papal Magisterium
            Against Slavery 75
Appendix C: Instructions of the Holy Office on Slavery 103
Appendix D: Pope John Paul II 117
Select Bibliography 121
Index 123

Foreword

The exceptional importance of diligent research and the mastery of primary sources is superbly illustrated by this little work, *The Popes and Slavery*. Most of the documentation contained in its Appendices is not readily accessible, and even less of it is accessible in English. As a result, an accurate history of the papacy's reaction to racial slavery has never been written, and what has been written is, in general, misleading.

As Fr. Panzer convincingly demonstrates, the reaction of the popes to racial slavery — from the time of its origins in the form that we generally recognize it — is what one would hope for and even expect. The popes, speaking for the entire Catholic Church as chief shepherds, vigorously condemned both racial slavery and the slave trade in a whole series of explicit and courageous documents, dating from 1435 to 1890. Of special importance is the work of Paul III in three documents of seminal influence in 1537. It is to the glory of these men that they recognized the evil of slavery and did not hesitate to cry out against it when so much of the Christian world was deaf and dumb.

If *The Popes and Slavery* indirectly reflects on the great gift Christ has given His Church in the ministry of Peter and his successors, it also illustrates the limitations of the papal office. The teaching of the popes on racial slavery was largely ignored for centuries by bishops, clergy and laity of the Church. The efforts of some of the American bishops, previous to the Civil War, to show how the papal teaching did not apply to the situation in the United States, is a very sorrowful chapter in the history of the Church in our country.

Fr. Panzer's ground-breaking work needs to be complemented. His insights to the differences between "just-title servitude" and racial slavery carry a profound significance, but we now need an equally diligent monograph — with documentation — on that type of servitude, arising as it did from the plight of prisoners of war and indentured servants. And, in addition, we require a study of even greater depth and greater difficulty: the social, cultural and economic milieu that surround such servitude. We require an analysis, too, of the influence of the papal condemnation of racial slavery on the theologians (de Vitoria is a shining example) of imperial Spain and its colonial governors and ministers. Without such studies, *The Popes and Slavery* remains but an isolated — even if very lustrous — start on a large canvas. But a start it is, well-documented, scholarly, and destined to play no small role in the development of the wider perspective.

Fr. James T. O'Connor

Preface

"I believe that unarmed truth and unconditional love will have the final word in reality. That is why right, temporarily defeated, is stronger than evil triumphant." These words are from the speech Dr. Martin Luther King, Jr. gave in accepting the Nobel Peace Prize in 1964. The many great speeches of this civil rights leader spoke volumes for the United States as it struggled to bring an end to legalized racism. However, this quotation in particular could be applied to a much larger expression of sanctioned racism, one that held much of the entire world in its grasp for over four and a half centuries, that of legalized racial slavery.

From the 1400's to the end of the last century, the practice of stealing the freedom of human beings of certain races and making them the servants of others was an evil that was allowed to dominate many societies. The Catholic Church had at her disposal only the weapons of truth and love to combat this evil — the truth of her teaching that all people are created equally by God, and loved unconditionally. That love has shown itself most clearly in the freedom and redemption won for us by Christ Jesus. The effects of this freedom and redemption from sin show themselves not only in eternity, but should be visible in many different ways in this life as well. How fitting it would seem, then, that the Catholic Church should have been a leader in the struggle to end the evil of slavery.

And yet many have posited that the Church did not provide such needed leadership to oppose slavery, and in many cases actually approved of the institution. This book is an attempt to discover the truth about the teaching of the Church on the issue of slavery. Its importance for the reader will not, I hope, be limited to lovers

of history and apologetics. As Dr. King himself stated, "We are not makers of history. We are made by history." The mistakes and advances of the past always have an effect on the future, and the historical events surrounding the Church and slavery certainly have value for our situation today. Perhaps the reader will discover the similarities of the past with the present, the tremendous gift the Church has in the office of the Papacy, and the need today more than ever for strong, courageous leadership from the Catholic hierarchy, and for reverent obedience and active involvement on the part of the Catholic faithful.

I want to express my gratitude to the staff of Corrigan Memorial Library of St. Joseph's Seminary, Yonkers, NY, and in particular to Mrs. Barbara Carey for her time and great patience, to Ms. Terri Rickel of the Love Library staff at the University of Nebraska, Lincoln, and to Mrs. Linda Way for proofreading the galleys. I also wish to thank Fr. James T. O'Connor, my former instructor at St. Joseph's Seminary, for his consistent priestly and scholarly example of true faith seeking understanding. He is certainly one who has touched the lives, thinking and ministries of myself and literally hundreds of priests before me. To have been able to study under such a man was a great gift indeed. This work is dedicated to Msgr. Leonard Kalin, the long-time chaplain of the Newman Center at the University of Nebraska and vocations director for the Diocese of Lincoln, to whom in a very real way, next to Christ and Our Lady, I owe my vocation to the sacred priesthood.

Father Joel S. Panzer

THE POPES AND SLAVERY

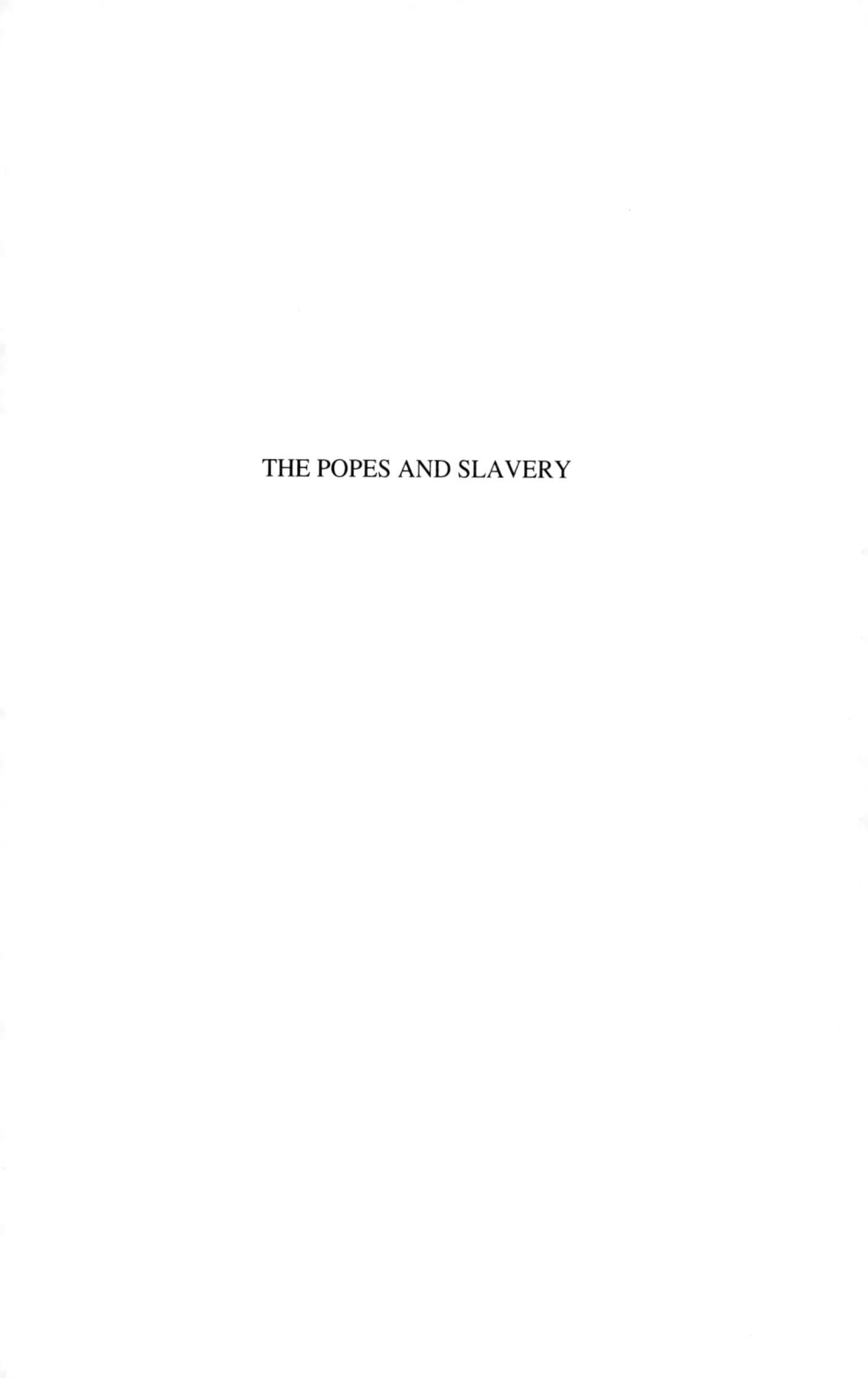

CHAPTER ONE

The State of the Question

In the American movie, *The Mission* (1986), there is told the historically-based story of the suppression and near extinction of a group of native South American Indians. Their destiny was played out amid the background of the Spanish and Portuguese rivalry in the New World, and the chicanery of some of the highest placed clergy of the Catholic Church. Spain had already eliminated the slave trade, but Portugal had not. In the name of profit the Spanish-held territory in which the Indians lived was traded for non-occupied Portuguese lands, allowing Portugal to sell enslavement "rights" on the newly acquired territory to slave traders. *The Mission* portrays the struggle between the Indians and their missionaries on the one hand, and the Portuguese political and ecclesiastical authorities on the other. The differing approaches that Spain and Portugal and their missionary clergy took towards the fate of the indigenous peoples in the 18th century (the time frame of the movie) actually had a history that extends back to the discovery of the Americas. These differing policies are reflected in the subjugation of the native Americans, and later, the black Africans who were brought to the colonies and sold as slaves.

    It is a sad history, filled with the greed and cruelty of colonizers and the venality and cowardice of churchmen. There are bright spots, however, as evidenced by those clergy and politicians who fought to defend the natives and to prohibit the enslavement of the Africans. Their efforts were often frustrated. In Portuguese

Brazil and in North America, legal slavery lasted until the 19th century; in Spanish America, where the laws were good, the implementation and enforcement was quite otherwise.

The contrasting attitudes of Spain and Portugal, both Catholic countries, and of various members of the clergy, are factors involved in the contemporary discussion concerning the Catholic Church's attitude towards slavery. When did the Catholic Church condemn slavery? According to some notable figures, the Church did not finally condemn slavery until not long ago. Judge John T. Noonan states that it was not until 1890 that the Church condemned the institution of slavery.[1] He and others argue that slavery is one of the areas in which the Church has changed its moral teaching to suit the times, and that the time for this change did not come until near the end of the last century. Theologian Laennec Hurbon may be cited as representing a belief among many authors that no pope before 1890 condemned slavery when he states that, "...one can search in vain through the interventions of the Holy See — those of Pius V, Urban VIII and Benedict XIV — for any condemnation of the actual principle of slavery."[2] Author John F. Maxwell wrote in his 1975 work on slavery that the Church did not correct its teaching on the moral legitimacy of slavery until 1965, with the publication from the Second Vatican Council of the Constitution *Gaudium et Spes*.[3]

In fact, the popes have condemned what is commonly known

---

[1] "Only after the cultures of Europe and America changed through the abolitionists' agency and only after the laws of every civilized land eliminated the practice, did Catholic moral doctrine decisively repudiate slavery as immoral. Only in 1890 did Pope Leo XIII attack the institution itself, noting that slavery was incompatible 'with the brotherhood that unites all men'" (reference to Leo XIII, *Catholicae Ecclesiae*, November 20, 1890), John T. Noonan, Jr., "Development in Moral Doctrine," *Theological Studies* 54 (December 1993) 675.

[2] Laennec Hurbon, "The Church and Afro-American Slavery," *The Church in Latin America: 1492-1992*, ed. by Enrique Dussel (Maryknoll, NY: Orbis Books, 1992) 372.

[3] "As is well known the common teaching on slavery was officially corrected by the Second Vatican Council in 1965 [in *Gaudium et Spes*, nos. 27, 29]," John F. Maxwell, *Slavery and the Catholic Church* (Chichester: Ross, 1975) 11. This work is of course ground breaking, especially for the English-speaking world, and Fr. Maxwell dedicated several years of research to produce a sincere and complete study of the subject. However, it must be read with caution, since, apart from his interpretation of the events and documents, his factual information is not infrequently wrong.

as slavery from its beginnings in the 15th century. This was accomplished through the moral teaching authority of the pope, known as the Papal Magisterium. The earlier forms of servitude were varied, complex, and very often of a different sociological category than those which were prevalent after the 14th century. While all forms of servitude are certainly unacceptable to most people today, this has not always been the case. Formerly, the rules of war and society were such that servitude was often imposed as a penalty on criminals and prisoners of war, and was even freely chosen by many workers for economic reasons. Children born of those held in servitude were also at times considered to be in the same state as that of their parents. These types of servitude were the most common among those generally considered to establish the so-called "just titles" of servitude. In such cases, it must be noted that the Church was always adamant about the obligation of masters to give fair and humane treatment to those held in servitude, and even encouraged their liberation.

A word needs to be said about so-called "just title servitude." The law of nations and modern convictions no longer consider some of the "just titles" of former ages to be appropriate pretexts for servitude. For example, some nations no longer allow the enforced servitude of criminals, and indentured servitude and other economically motivated forms of the institution are not acceptable in most societies today. Even so, the Geneva Conventions of 1949 still allow for a detaining power to utilize the labor of prisoners of war.[4] We do not want to ignore, or give moral approbation to, the abuses and terrible injustices that were often the unfortunate result of just title servitude. Indeed, some of the most extreme cases of this abuse involved enslavement through deceptive uses of the just titles. However, would it be possible to say that such former practices are *intrinsically* wrong? Certainly, the capital form of criminal pun-

---

[4] See *Geneva Convention Relative to the Treatment of Prisoners of War of August 12, 1949*, Part III, Section III, Article 49. To prevent abuses of human rights, the servitude of prisoners of war is heavily restricted in terms of type of work expected, working conditions, risk of injury, duration of daily labor and even contains the requirement that remuneration be given for the work done (cf. Articles 50-57).

ishment practiced even today — the death penalty — would be more extreme than the former practice of penal servitude. To the surprise of many, the Church continues to uphold the *objective* right of the State to impose the death penalty, although the times when such a right might be justifiably exercised are taught to be, practically speaking, nonexistent.[5] Likewise, in the poverty of previous times most people would have preferred to have the basic necessities of life met, such as having enough food to eat — though it was earned in freely chosen service to another — than to starve in their liberty. In fact, some clearly undesirable forms of such servitude exist even today, and even in the United States, as the condition of many immigrants and other foreign workers makes evident.

We need a detailed study of this so-called just title servitude, especially since it is so often lumped together with what we normally call slavery. However, such instances are very different from that type of servitude which had no moral foundation whatsoever; in fact, Pope Paul III in 1537 described this latter form of servitude as "unheard of before now."[6] Starting in the first half of the 15th century, Spain and Portugal initiated the so-called Age of Discovery, although it is well to remember — as Francisco de Vitoria noted — the native Americans did not need discovering; they knew where they were.[7] To the peoples residing in the territories that were discovered by the Europeans came not only the good news of Christ's Gospel, but also for many the evil of enslavement, since it quickly became the practice to force into servitude many of the peoples who were found to be living in these lands. Indeed it was common practice for such atrocities to be committed under the guise of the Gospel, as the argument was often made that the only way to bring the Christian faith to them was by brute force and human subjection. Clearly, slavery of this form differed not only in degree, but also in nature, from the just titles described above since the justifying motive for this type of servitude was either

---

[5] John Paul II, *Evangelium Vitae*, No. 56.

[6] Paul III, *Sublimis Deus*, see Appendix B, No. 2.

[7] *The New Encyclopedia Britannica* (Chicago: Encyclopedia Britannica, Inc., 1985) s.v. "Vitoria, Francisco de," by B.M.H., 405.

bogus or non-existent. This subjection came about not because those so treated were prisoners of war or criminals or indentured servants or born into servitude, but rather was enforced on people out of an immoral desire for cheap human labor. Furthermore, there is a distinctive racial element in this kind of slavery. Although not totally absent anywhere in previous types of servitude, it is most noticeable after the European discoveries in Africa and the New World.

There existed of course the practice of various types of unjust servitude or slavery before the 15th century, and these were certainly not held by the Church to be acceptable. This practice was prevalent, as far as can be determined, in all societies, including Africa and the Americas — and an examination should be made of that period of history. However, it was not until the 15th century, and with growing frequency from the 16th to the 19th centuries, that such unjust slavery became dominant.[8] It is this form of servitude that is called to mind when we think today of the institution of slavery, and is the type which was to prevail in parts of the New World for over four centuries.

We have been using above the words, "servitude" and "slavery." Both words are possible translations of the Latin "*servitus.*" When speaking of the *servitus* which rested on one of the so-called "just titles," we translate the Latin as "servitude"; when speaking of that form of *servitus* which did not rest on just title, we translate the Latin as "slavery." In the Magisterial documents that we will be considering, the institution of slavery is referred to by such Latin phrases as *servituti subicere* (to *subject* to slavery), or, more commonly, *in servitutem redigere* (to *reduce* to slavery). By the use of

---

[8] *The New Catholic Encyclopedia* (Washington: Catholic University of America, 1967), s.v. "Slavery (History of)," by C. Verlinden, 284, 286.

[9] Maxwell evidently does not accept the distinction between the just titles to servitude that were upheld, and the particular forms of slavery which first developed, and were first condemned, in the 15th century: "Since the sixth century and right up until the twentieth century it has been common Catholic teaching that the social, economic and legal institution of slavery is morally legitimate provided that the master's title of ownership is valid and provided that the slave is properly looked after and cared for, both materially and spiritually" (*Slavery*, 10). This allows him to suggest a questionable thesis: "...for over 1,400 years the Church's fallible ordinary magisterium was mistaken in its interpretation of the natural moral law concerning the institution of slavery..." (*Slavery*, 13).

such terms, the documents are referring to *servitus* in its unjust and most commonly understood form.[9]

This brings us back to the question: When did the Church condemn this type of slavery? If it was not until 1890, or even 1965, then a great shadow is indeed cast upon the Magisterium. If, however, it can be shown that the Magisterium condemned from the beginning the colonial slavery that developed in the newly discovered lands, then it may be necessary for some historians, theologians and others to revise their opinions of the Church's official record on the issue of slavery.

We will address the responses of the Papal Magisterium to the widespread enslavement that accompanied the Age of Discovery and beyond. From 1435 to 1890 we have numerous bulls and encyclicals from several popes written to many bishops and the whole Christian faithful condemning both slavery and the slave trade. The very existence of these many papal teachings during this particular period of history is a strong indication that from the viewpoint of the Magisterium there must have developed a moral problem of a different sort than any previously encountered in respect to servitude.

Thus, we wish here to make available and reflect upon those works that comprise the teaching of the Papal Magisterium on racial slavery, from the beginning of the European territorial finds until the end of the last century. Our consideration will consist of presenting a brief history of each of the popes who authored documents on slavery, an examination of the content of each of the documents, and a limited commentary on the implications of each of these teachings. The appendices provide both Latin and English texts of the papal documents and of some relevant instructions of the Holy Office. It is to these works that we now turn in an effort to understand better this pivotal aspect of the Church's record on the issue of slavery.

CHAPTER TWO

Papal Teachings on Slavery

THE FIRST HUNDRED YEARS
(1435-1536)

Eugene IV: *Sicut Dudum,* January 13, 1435

Eugene IV was born in Venice c. 1383, named Gabriele Condulmaro, and served as the Bishop of Rome from March 3, 1431 to February 23, 1447. A pious man who strengthened the hand of the papacy at the close of the age of conciliarism, Eugene nevertheless suffered many embarrassments and setbacks. Notably, he was forced to flee a revolution in Rome, due to his suppression of the corrupt activities of the vindictive Colonna family, and to take up residence in Florence for nine years thereafter (1434-1443).[10]

An effort for which Eugene should not be ashamed is his issuing from Florence the bull *Sicut Dudum* on January 13, 1435.[11] Sent to Bishop Ferdinand, located at Rubicon on the island of Lanzarote, this bull condemned the enslavement of the Guanches and other peoples of the newly colonized Canary Islands. After

---

[10] J.N.D. Kelly, *The Oxford Dictionary of the Popes* (Oxford: Oxford University Press, 1986), 241-243.

[11] Maxwell cites a 1433 Bull of Eugene IV, *Cum Aliquando* (Baronius, *Annales Ecclesiastici*, ed. O. Raynaldus, Luca, 1752, vol. 28, n. 25, 225), as also condemning the enslavement of the people of the Canaries (Maxwell, *Slavery*, 51), but this earlier work of Eugene is in fact not concerned with the issue of slavery.

being converted to the faith or promised baptism, many of the inhabitants were taken from their home and enslaved by the Europeans:

> They have deprived the natives of their property or turned it to their own use, and have subjected some of the inhabitants of said islands to perpetual slavery (*subdiderunt perpetuae servituti*), sold them to other persons and committed other various illicit and evil deeds against them... Therefore We... exhort, through the sprinkling of the Blood of Jesus Christ shed for their sins, one and all, temporal princes, lords, captains, armed men, barons, soldiers, nobles, communities and all others of every kind among the Christian faithful of whatever state, grade or condition, that they themselves desist from the aforementioned deeds, cause those subject to them to desist from them, and restrain them rigorously. And no less do We order and command all and each of the faithful of each sex that, within the space of fifteen days of the publication of these letters in the place where they live, that they restore to their earlier liberty all and each person of either sex who were once residents of said Canary Islands... who have been made subject to slavery (*servituti subicere*). These people are to be totally and perpetually free and are to be let go without the exaction or reception of any money.[12]

The date of this Bull, 1435, is very significant. Nearly sixty years before the Europeans were to find the New World, we already have the papal condemnation of slavery as soon as this crime was discovered in one of the first of the Portuguese geographical discoveries. Eugene IV is clear in his intentions both to condemn the enslavement of the residents of the Canary Islands, and to demand correction of the injustice within fifteen days. Those who do not restore the enslaved to their liberty in that time incur the sentence of excommunication *ipso facto*.

As noted, many believe it was not long ago that the Catholic

---
[12] See Appendix B, No. 1.

Church condemned slavery. However, it was in fact quite a long time ago, about five hundred and sixty years back, with the issuance of *Sicut Dudum*, that the Church through the Papal Magisterium began its battle to condemn the unjust enslavement of free peoples. Nonetheless, this abuse of human liberty was to plague Africa and the Western Hemisphere until the later part of the last century.

Any future efforts to enslave the peoples of the Canaries is also condemned under pain of the same penalty:

> We will that like sentence of excommunication be incurred by one and all who attempt to capture or sell or subject to slavery (*servituti subicere*) baptized residents of the Canary Islands or those who are freely seeking Baptism..."[13]

Though the Bull limits itself here to those baptized or desiring baptism, it is doubtful that the people outside of the Christian faith were somehow not meant to be included in the future protection from enslavement commanded by Eugene IV. Rather, the Pope was likely under the assumption that most of the natives forced by deceit and trickery into slavery were those who had had previous contact with the Christians, and so were either baptized or wished to be so. The words of the instruction stating that all of the residents of the Canary Islands taken captive be freed are enough to prove that enslavement of any of these peoples, Christian or non-Christian, is forbidden.

Some may be inclined to argue that the wording of this document is such that the particular action of making the people of the Canary Islands slaves is condemned, but that the actual principle of slavery itself is not condemned. However, this argument fails to convince when we consider both the tone and content of the letter. The enslavement of the natives is spoken of as being "illicit and evil." Subjecting one to slavery is condemned as illicit. Eugene states that he is writing "with sorrow." Mention is made of the

---

[13] *Ibid.*, No. 1.

obvious negative effect that this enslavement will have on the Christian religion in the Canaries. Lastly, but perhaps most importantly, this evil is considered worthy of the penalty of excommunication in its second highest form. In this we might compare it to the Church's modern teaching on abortion, which is also accompanied by the same type of excommunication.

With *Sicut Dudum*, Eugene was clearly intending to condemn the enslavement of the people of the Canaries and, in no uncertain terms, to inform the faithful that what was being condemned was what in today's terminology would be called gravely wrong. Thus, the unjust racial slavery that had begun in the newly found territories was condemned, condemned as soon as it was discovered, and condemned in the strongest of terms. Subsequent bulls were issued by Pius II and Sixtus IV in defense of the residents of the Canary Islands, who were still being enslaved at the hands of the Christians. In the *Annales Ecclesiastici*, we have the commentary of Baronius on these two bulls (no extant copy of the actual text of this section of Pius II's Bull is available), both penalizing the Europeans who were leading the newly baptized into slavery.[14]

The very existence of these, and many subsequent papal teachings, shows that what was taught was frequently not accepted by the European Christians operating in Africa and the New World. Such a chasm between teaching and practice is certainly not without historical precedence in a Church whose members are tainted by the effects of original sin. In our own century as well, the words of Peter's successors are often rendered little more than verbal assent, at times even by those entrusted with the task of making that teaching a reality in society. For example, the constant teaching of the popes from *Rerum Novarum* of Leo XIII to *Centesimus Annus* of John Paul II has been that workers have a natural right to form the professional associations of tradesmen we commonly call labor unions. Yet Catholic hospitals, schools and other institutions have been among the most hesitant to permit their establishment.

---

[14] *Annales Ecclesiastici*, Vol. 29, n. 42, 342, Vol. 29, n. 21, 575.

We know that Christ guarantees that the Church will teach the truth, but whether her clerics and laity will give internal assent and obedience to that truth is a separate matter. Pope Eugene's efforts on behalf of the peoples of the Canary Islands were merely the first in a long struggle to direct the world away from the sinful greed that was at the heart of slavery, a greed that allowed that institution to be perpetuated across three continents in well over four centuries.

Alexander VI: *Eximiae Devotionis,* May 4, 1493
Inter Caetera, May 4, 1493
Ineffabilis et Summi Patris, June 1, 1497

Rodrigo de Borgia y Borgia was born in Spain January 1, 1431. He was endowed to an extreme by his nepotist uncle, Pope Callistus III, with numerous bishoprics and abbeys, so that at age twenty-six he was thought to be the second wealthiest cardinal in the Church. He maintained the family tradition of nepotism after he successfully acquired the Chair of Peter on August 11, 1492, taking the name Alexander VI. Bribery, cronyism and promiscuity had marked his life previous to becoming pope, and not all of them disappeared after his election. He is, however, also noted for his attempts at reforming the Church, addressing some of the problems of the monasteries, but never those of the papacy. Also, Alexander financed expeditions during this Age of Discovery, and exercised concern for the missions in the New World. He died on August 18, 1503.[15]

The three mentioned letters of Alexander VI are not directly concerned with slavery, but, issued as they are at the start of the European territorial finds in the New World, contain the foundation of an essential teaching regarding the welfare of the native peoples. *Eximiae Devotionis* bestows on Spain various grants, privileges, etc. that had previously been given to Portugal. *Inter Caetera*

---

[15] Kelly, *Popes*, 252-254.

praises King Ferdinand and Queen Isabella for their tireless work for the faith, and notes, at the same time, that they sent Christopher Columbus, a "man worthy and highly to be commended, one suitable for the task,"[16] to discover remote and unknown lands. Columbus reported that he informed the people who dwelt in those lands of the existence of God, and that there was hope that they would accept the Christian faith. Since it is the stated intention of the King and Queen to bring the faith to these lands, islands and peoples, the Pope, as Vicar of Christ, grants them dominion over all the lands existing three hundred miles to the west of the Azores, trusting that they will fulfill their word to send good and learned men to lead the peoples there to the faith.[17]

In the above letter the Pope seems to be simply "giving away" the New World to Spain. Now, in fact, it was a common enough practice at that time for explorers to declare newly found lands to be the dominion of their rulers, but actually this is not what the Pope was doing for Spain. The Bull *Inter Caetera* was modified by the

---

[16] Alexander VI, *Inter Caetera* (Found in *Coleccion de Bulas, Breves y Otros Documentos Relativos a la Iglesia de America y Filipinas*), ed. by El. P. Francisco Javier Hernaez, S.J., Tome I, (Brussels, 1879); Reprinted by Kraus Reprint Ltd. (Vaduz, 1964), 12: "... *virum utique dignum et plurimum commendandum, ac tanto negotio aptum ...*"

[17] *Ibid.*, 12-14. Maxwell cites May 3, 1493 for this bull and says it gives to Spain the same grants received earlier by Portugal (*Slavery*, 55-56). This earlier "version" is probably a preparatory draft of the final copy.

Bartolome de Las Casas, impressed with the evangelization fostered by *Inter Caetera*, ordered it to be distributed in Mexico, and later used it in his writings (See Gustavo Gutierrez, *Las Casas: In Search of the Poor of Jesus Christ*, Maryknoll, NY: Orbis Books, 1993, 72). The following 16th century citation, thought by most scholars to be from the writings of Las Casas, tells how the Bull *Inter Caetera* of Alexander VI was understood:

"The Indians are free, ... and this is the conclusion arrived at in view of the Bull of the grant, made to the Sovereigns of Castile and León by Pope Alexander VI, of the said Indies and Mainland, as well as in consideration of a passage in the testament of our Most Serene Queen, of happy memory, in which she commends to the Catholic King, her consort, enjoining the same on his successors, a fair treatment of the said Indians, along with their farms, as these are free persons, so that they may be drawn to our holy Catholic faith." (*Las Casas*, note 8, 489). Citation taken from *Coleccion de documentos ineditors relativos al descubrimiento, conquista y organizacion de las antiguas posesiones espanolas de America y Oceania, sacados de los archivos del reino y muy especialmente del de Indias* (Madrid: 1864-84), Vol. 12, p. 107.

Treaty of Tordesillas (June 7, 1494) because the Portuguese complained that all the new territories were being given to Spain alone. Alexander thus granted Portugal the rights that would ultimately give them Brazil and other territories. However, the Pope in his letter to Portugal is more specific about what he in fact intends to do by his letters. He is not giving the New World away; he is giving to Spain and Portugal the rights to bring Christianity to these lands *on the presumption that the peoples of those lands freely choose the Kings of Spain and Portugal as their sovereigns.*[18]

That this is the case can be seen in the second letter of Alexander VI to King Emmanuel of Portugal, *Ineffabilis et Summi Patris*, June 1, 1497. Alexander mentions the King's request, which comes to him through the Portuguese Cardinal Gregory, that the Pope confirm the King's dominion over the newly-discovered territories, the purpose of this dominion being to extend the faith. The Pope notes the value of the request and grants the privilege conditionally:

> "... if it has happened that certain cities, camps, lands, places or dominions of the peoples without faith *have wished to be subject to you*, pay tribute to you and recognize you as their Sovereign" [emphasis added].[19]

---

[18] Maxwell believes that *Inter Caetera* and *Eximiae Devotionis* gave Spain and Portugal the right to make war on and enslave the peoples of the New World:
"...both Monarchies received the identical authority to treat their newly discovered territory in the same way that they could receive authority from the Pope to treat, say, Turkey or Egypt: that is to say, they received 'full and free permission to invade, search out, capture and subjugate the Saracens and pagans and any other unbelievers and enemies of Christ... and to reduce their persons into perpetual slavery.' In other words, it would appear that, in effect, Portugal and Spain were understood by the Holy See to be at war with the Negroes of West Africa and the 'Indians' of America" (*Slavery*, 56).

Maxwell has in fact made an invalid jump from a 1454 Brief of Pope Nicholas V to King Alfonso V, to the 1493 Briefs of Alexander VI. The 1454 brief was concerned with the waging of just wars against the very real enemies of the Catholic Church, and should not be interpreted to apply to peoples in lands who were not at war with the Christian nations. In fact, *Inter Caetera* makes no mention of making war on other nations or peoples.

[19] Hernaez, *Coleccion*, II, 836: "... *si forsan contingeret aliquas Civitates, castra, terras, et loca seu Dominia Infidelium ditioni tuae subjici, seu tributum solvere, et te in eorum Dominum cognoscere velle. ....*"

The Pope stressed this point by repeating it in the next paragraph of the letter, when he accedes to the King's request:

> "By the authority granted us by Almighty God in St. Peter and by Apostolic authority, we confirm for you and your successors dominion over said cities, camps, places, lands and dominions which, as was said before, have had occasion *to wish to be subject to you*, pay tribute to you and recognize you as their Sovereign" [emphasis added].[20]

Thus it is quite clear that Alexander VI's intention was not simply to give away other people's lands, but rather to give Spain and Portugal the authority of the Church to bring both the Catholic faith and their own countries' civil authority *to those peoples who are freely willing to accept them*. At this early date after the European discovery of the New World, the Pope already was concerned about maintaining the free will of the Indians. His successors would soon be stressing this freedom when it came to discerning between just and unjust servitude, and the immorality of reducing the Indians to slavery. It is interesting to note that Hernaez alone provides us with this important document. He likewise notes in his commentary the significance of the teaching of *Ineffabilis et Summi Patris* concerning the freedom of the Indians.[21]

---

[20] *Ibid.*, 837: "... *auctoritate Omnipotentis Dei Nobis in Beato Petro concessa, de Civitatibus, castris, locis, terris, et Dominiis praedictis, quae tibi ditionique tuae, ut praefertur, subjici, quae te in Dominum cognoscere, seu tributum solvere velle contigerit...*"

Maxwell fails to realize the true intentions of Alexander VI because he is apparently unaware of the existence of *Ineffabilis et Summi Patris*. He instead misinterprets the meaning of Alexander's letters, as noted above.

[21] *Ibid.*, 837. In this, Hernaez is agreeing with Las Casas's own interpretation of *Inter Caetera*, arrived at without apparent knowledge of *Ineffabilis et Summi Patris*: "Las Casas goes further still. It is not enough that the Pope grant the dominion: The Indians must freely accept it" (Gutierrez, *Las Casas*, 379; see p. 389 as well).

THE SECOND HUNDRED YEARS
(1537-1638)

After realizing the existence of the peoples of the New World, some Europeans questioned whether these seemingly barbarous inhabitants were in fact human or subhuman. If they were not rational men capable of receiving the faith, then some believed such unconvertible infidels could be conquered. Debates ensued in which the natives were held by some to be of a category of people who were "slaves by nature," a theory first pondered by Aristotle in his *Politics*. In the end, the Spanish decided in the Laws of Burgos (December 27, 1512) that the Indians were indeed able to be made Christians, and ambitious programs for their conversion were initiated.[22] Sadly, it was soon to be argued fallaciously that, in the name of those conversions, the inhabitants could be justly conquered and enslaved, not because they were slaves by nature, but because they would not peaceably accept the Christians and their faith. It was in response to such abuses of religious and human rights that Bartolome de Las Casas began his extended endeavors to evangelize and protect the Indians in Mexico.

---

[22] Hugh Thomas, *Conquest: Montezuma, Cortes, and the Fall of Old Mexico* (New York: Simon and Schuster, 1993), 71.

It should be noted that the practice of slavery in the New World did not begin with the Europeans; it was a common practice amongst many American tribes, especially in war. Of slavery in Mexico, Hugh Thomas writes:

"In the classification of these ancient Mexicans, there were a few real slaves... they could own property, buy their liberty, and marry free women or men... Many of these slaves were *macehualtin* who had committed crimes or who had failed to meet levies for tribute; peasants who had become slaves when sold by families who needed food... Some too were people who had made themselves slaves voluntarily, to escape the responsibilities of normal life."

Though this sounds much like the just titles to servitude practiced in Europe, Thomas notes a difference regarding the Mexican slaves: "But there was one serious disadvantage: they could be sacrificed" (*Conquest*, 35).

Paul III

Alessandro Farnese was born on February 29, 1468, and served as visible head of the Church from October 13, 1534 to November 10, 1549. He was well educated in the liberal arts and well financed from Church bishoprics and benefices, but was not ordained until 1519. While himself leading an immoral life before ordination, as Pope he nevertheless worked diligently to reform the state of the Church, calling the Council of Trent in 1545.[23]

Hernaez states in his *Coleccion* that, previous to the issuance of the antislavery teachings of Paul III, the Catholic kings had been attempting to convert and exercise dominion over the Indians by peaceable means.[24] These attempts quickly gave way to the use of force, however. Frustrated that the Spanish and Portuguese had resorted so soon to violence in their efforts to make inroads in these territories, the Dominican missionaries, and especially Las Casas, redirected their efforts from Seville to Rome. There they implored the assistance of Pope Paul III.[25]

Sublimis Deus, June 2, 1537

The pontifical decree known as *The Sublime God* has indeed played an exalted role in the cause of social justice in the New World. Recently, authors such as Gustavo Gutierrez have noted this fact: "The bull of Pope Paul III, *Sublimis Deus* (June 2, 1537), is regarded as the most important papal pronouncement on the human condition of the Indians."[26] Moreover, it is addressed to all of the Christian faithful in the world, and not to a particular bishop in one area, thereby not limiting its significance, but universalizing it.

According to Helen Rand Parish, *Sublimis Deus* went through

---

[23] Kelly, *Popes*, 261-262.
[24] Hernaez, *Coleccion*, I, 102.
[25] Gutierrez, *Las Casas*, 302-305.
[26] *Ibid.*, 302.

at least one draft in its development. The document often cited as *Veritas Ipsa*[27] is, it would appear, an earlier draft, which lacks the introductory paragraph of *Sublimis*, and has other small differences. *Veritas* was going to be issued as a papal letter. It was decided, however, to elevate it to the status of a Bull with an improved preamble and other slight changes.[28] This would explain the same date of the two works (June 2, 1537), as well as the confusion that exists among authors, some of whom believe them to be two separate documents. At any rate, *Sublimis* does not vary from *Veritas* in any substantial way, nor do the various versions of *Sublimis* differ significantly from Parish's critical edition issued recently.

Sublimis Deus was intended to be issued as the central pedagogical work against slavery. Two other bulls would be published to implement the teaching of *Sublimis*, one to impose penalties on those who failed to abide by the teaching against slavery, and a second to specify the sacramental consequences of the teaching that the Indians are truly human beings.[29] However, because the Feast of Corpus Christi fell on the weekend *Sublimis* was to be issued, it was not signed until the following Monday, three days after the other two.[30]

---

[27] See Appendix B, No. 3.

[28] Helen Rand Parish and Harold E. Weidman, *Las Casas en Mexico: Historia y obras desconocidas* (Mexico: Fondo de Cultura Economica, 1992) note 7, 84. Due to Parish's invaluable work, Gutierrez is led to note that "Today, thanks to Helen Rand Parish, we have a better knowledge of what actually occurred. In her recent *Las Casas en Mexico*, the illustrious historian has shed light on little-known aspects of the life and work of Las Casas on the basis of unpublished documents" (Gutierrez, *Las Casas*, 303).

[29] Parish, *Las Casas en Mexico*, 18; note 8c, 84. That *Sublimis* is the primary or governing document, the others executing, was seen by Las Casas himself, in his use of the documents in his *The Only Way* (*De Unico Modo*), when he updated it:
"Finally, we recall the papal encyclical 'God Who is beyond us,' which insists on peaceful conversion. The High Priest and Vicar of Christ Himself gave teeth to that decree [*Sublimis Deus*] when he made the archbishop of Toledo the judge and executor of it. The archbishop was in Toledo at the time. The Pope gave him complete power to force the tyrants not to injure, not to oppress the Indians as they had done against every law. And power to give relief directly to the Indians concerning their freedom and ownership or their own goods."
(Bartolome de las Casas, *The Only Way*, ed. by Helen Rand Parish, Trans. by Francis Patrick Sullivan, S.J. (Mahwah, N.J.: Paulist Press, 1992), 156).

[30] Parish, *Las Casas en Mexico*, 18; note 7, 84.

Parish notes the difficulty she encountered in both Rome and Seville in finding copies of the originals of *Sublimis Deus* and *Pastorale Officium* for her critical editions.[31] In fact, *Sublimis* became completely unknown to most people after the 17th century, and was often referred to in its draft form, *Veritas Ipsa*. These and other factors have led to much confusion surrounding *Sublimis*, and have resulted in its relative infrequent mention by older authors.[32]

The first and central teaching of this beautiful work is the universality of the call to receive the faith and salvation:

> And since mankind, according to the witness of Sacred Scripture, was created for eternal life and happiness and since no one is able to attain this eternal life and happiness except through faith in our Lord Jesus Christ, it is necessary to confess that man is of such a nature and condition that he is capable of receiving faith in Christ and that everyone who possesses human nature is apt for receiving such faith... Therefore the Truth Himself Who can neither deceive nor be deceived, when He destined the preachers of the faith to the office of preaching, is known to have said: "Going, make disciples of all nations." "All," he said, without any exception since all are capable of the discipline of the faith.[33]

---

[31] *Ibid.*, 18; note 8, 84-85. Though Parish states that her's is the first critical edition of *Sublimis Deus*, Francis MacNutt also provided the Latin text of the Bull in his *Bartholomew De Las Casas: His Life, His Apostolate, and His Writings* (New York: G.P. Putnam's Sons, 1909), 426-430. MacNutt had reprinted the Latin, with slight variations and some misspellings, from a work by Carlo Gutierrez entitled *Fray Bartolome de las Casas: Sus Tiempos y Su Apostolado*.

[32] Denzinger cites Paul III's *Pastorale Officium* on slavery (DS 1495), and Hernaez provides the text of *Veritas Ipsa* (*Coleccion*, I, 102-103), but interestingly, neither author makes reference to *Sublimis Deus* itself. Neither does the new *Denzinger-Huenermann* (Rome: Herder, 1991, DH 1495).

Furthermore, *Sublimis* and its draft version, as well as the other works, are frequently misdated. For example: John Eppstein dates *Sublimis* as June 17 instead of June 2 (*The Catholic Tradition of the Law of Nations*, London: Burns, Oates and Washbourne, Ltd., 1935, 420); in the footnotes of *In Plurimis*, the Acta Sanctae Sedes misdates *Veritas* as 1559 instead of 1537, and *In Supremo* is misdated as 1837 instead of 1839 (20:555). The same errors are true of the *Acta Leonis XIII* (3:80, 81) and *The Papal Encyclicals* of Claudia Carlen (2:167).

[33] See Appendix B, No. 2.

The sole qualification for receiving the faith is contained in that common quality of all the different peoples of the world, namely, the possession of human nature.[34] While this theme that salvation is attainable by all people is found also in *Pastorale Officium*, dated four days earlier, it should be noted that the weight of *Sublimis* is greater since it is addressed to all the faithful, and that *Sublimis* was intended as the foundational document from which *Pastorale* and other instructional briefs were developed.

The teaching of *Sublimis* continues:

> Seeing this and envying it, the enemy of the human race, who always opposes all good men so that the race may perish, has thought up a way, unheard of before now, by which he might impede the saving word of God from being preached to the nations. He has stirred up some of his allies who, desiring to satisfy their own avarice, are presuming to assert far and wide that the Indians of the West and the South who have come to our notice in these times be reduced to our service like brute animals, under the pretext that they are lacking the Catholic faith. And they reduce them to slavery (*Et eos in servitutem redigunt*), treating them with afflictions they would scarcely use with brute animals.[35]

The common pretext of the allies of "the enemy of the human race," i.e. Satan, for enslaving the Indians was that they lacked the faith. Some of the Europeans used the reasoning that converting the Indians should be accomplished by any means necessary, thus making the faith an excuse for war and enslavement. Paul III states that

---

[34] Aware of the tremendous value of the teaching of *Sublimis Deus* for the New World, John Tracy Ellis provides its translation in his *Documents of American Catholic History*. Of *Sublimis*, Ellis notes, "To combat the charge that the Indians were not capable of receiving the Catholic faith, Paul III... issued on June 2, 1537 the bull *Sublimis Deus*." *Documents*, I (Wilmington, Delaware: Michael Glazier, Inc., 1987), 7. The abuse of the Indians' religious liberty was, however, a mere corollary of the fundamental problem which Paul III sought to address. It should be remembered that the true purpose for issuing *Sublimis Deus* was to combat the unjust enslavement of the Indians.

[35] *Ibid.*, No. 2.

the practice of this form of servitude was "unheard of before now." This clearly indicates that the practice of enslaving an entire ethnic group of people — the Indians of South America — for no morally justifiable reason was indeed different from anything previously encountered. Soon, slavery in the New World and in Africa would be practiced without any effort to provide such excuses. But in the beginning at least, this new form of enslavement was accompanied by such vain attempts at justification. As mentioned above, others debated whether the Indians lacked a rational human nature, and thus were unable to come to a knowledge of God, or perhaps were even "slaves by nature." All of these arguments and theories are definitively rejected, since these newly found peoples are known by Paul III to be rational and human. In this regard, Hugh Thomas notes the influence the New World missionaries had in the issuing of *Sublimis Deus*:

> Julian Garces, who eventually became the first bishop of Tlaxcala [New Spain], wrote to Pope Paul III in 1535 praising the intelligence of the Mexican Indians, insisting that they were neither turbulent nor ungovernable, but reverent, shy and obedient to their teachers. The idea that they were incapable of receiving the doctrines of the church "surely had been prompted by the devil."[36]

The second core teaching of *Sublimis Deus* which follows from this is the necessity of restoring and maintaining the liberty of the Indians:

> Therefore, We, ... noting that the Indians themselves indeed are true men and are not only capable of the Christian faith, but, as has been made known to us, promptly hasten to the faith, and wishing to provide suitable remedies for them, by our Apostolic Authority decree and declare by these present letters that the same Indians and all other peoples — even though they are outside the faith — who shall hereafter come

---

[36] Thomas, *Conquest*, 590.

to the knowledge of Christians have not been deprived or should not be deprived of their liberty or of their possessions (*sua libertate ac rerum suarum dominio privatos seu privandos non esse*). Rather they are to be able to use and enjoy this liberty and this ownership of property freely and licitly, and are not to be reduced to slavery (*nec in servitutem redigi debere*), and that whatever happens to the contrary is to be considered null and void. These same Indians and other peoples are to be invited to the said faith in Christ by preaching and the example of a good life.[37]

Paul states that the Indians are "true men" who are able to accept the faith, and in fact do so eagerly. Thus, "the same Indians *and all other peoples* — even though they are *outside the faith*" (emphasis added),[38] are not to have their possessions taken or their lives reduced to slavery. In fact, Paul believes that there has not been any juridical deprivation of the rights of the Indians, nor should there be. By these words, Paul is teaching that he does not interpret *Inter Caetera* of Alexander VI to have given away the Indians rights to liberty and property, as we noted earlier.[39] This teaching is not to be limited to Christians or Indians only, and is to be applied to any and all peoples who may be encountered in the future. Anything done or taught contrary to this universal Bull is null and void. The conversion, not the domination, of the Indians is to be the goal of the Europeans; this goal is not to be attained by violence, but rather "by preaching and the example of a good life."[40]

---

[37] See Appendix B, No. 2.

[38] *Ibid.*, No. 2.

[39] See pages 11-14, and footnotes 17, 19 and 20. Gutierrez states that the 16th century writer Juan de la Pena understood *Sublimis Deus* in this same way:
"The first thing that Paul III defined in it was that those unbelievers, the Indians, were human beings with a capacity for eternal life and eternal death. The second thing that he defined was that those unbelievers have not been deprived *de facto*, nor should they be, of the ancient sovereignty that they have over their possessions. On the contrary, he commanded that they be allowed to make free use of them as their own." (*Las Casas*, note 33, 311). Citation taken from Juan de la Pena, *De Bello*, 1:193.

[40] See Appendix B, No. 2.

Pastorale Officium, May 29, 1537

Paul issued his chronologically first work on slavery, *Pastorale Officium*, on May 29, 1537, to Cardinal Juan de Tavera, Archbishop of Toledo. He intended to give ecclesiastical support to a Royal edict of Charles V of Spain issued seven years earlier forbidding any enslavement of the Indians in the new Spanish territories.[41] In *Pastorale*, Paul first praises the antislavery efforts of Charles, and then states:

> Therefore, attending to the fact that the Indians themselves, although they are outside the bosom of the Church, have not been and should not be deprived of their liberty or of ownership of what is their own, and that, since they are men and therefore capable of faith and salvation, they are not to be given into servitude (*servitute delendos*), but rather by preaching, good example and the like should be invited to [eternal] life, and wishing to repress the evil efforts of such bad men, lest worn out by injuries and harm, it be more difficult for the Indians to embrace faith in Christ, We... command that anyone of whatever dignity, state, condition or grade who works against what is done through you or others to help the Indians in the aforementioned matters incurs the penalty of excommunication *latae sententiae*, incurred *ipso facto*. This penalty is to be absolved only by Us or the Roman Pontiff then reigning, except in the case of impending death and with foreseen satisfaction. This is done so that no one in any way may presume to reduce said Indians to slavery (*in servitutem redigere*) or despoil them of their goods.[42]

This Brief is significant for two reasons. First, because it teaches, like *Sublimis Deus*, that non-Christian status does not in itself give

---

[41] Maxwell notes nevertheless that the 1530 Royal edict, *Cedulario Indiano*, had stated that the Indians themselves practiced enslavement of their prisoners of war (*Slavery*, 58-59).

[42] *Ibid.*, No. 4. Maxwell refers to a slightly different version of *Pastorale* dated June 2, 1537 (*Slavery*, 69). This second version is not known to exist, but if it does, it may be a rough draft that was mistakenly thought to be a later edition.

any moral justification for enslavement. Secondly, because it states in line with *Sublimis* specifically that the Indians are men who thus have the ability to come to a knowledge of the Faith, and are not, as some believed, brute and irrational animals. *Pastorale* was given the strongest ecclesial backing possible, by the attachment of a *latae sententiae* excommunication remittable solely by the Holy Father. Additionally, the Archbishop of Toledo was mandated to do whatever else he deemed necessary to protect the Indians in this regard.

By 1537 Charles, however, had already revoked his edict — doing so in 1534 — because of the difficulties some of the colonies were experiencing. Once again, the enslavement of Indian prisoners of war was permitted. This revocation Paul must have obviously not known when he wrote *Pastorale* in 1537, and at the request of the Emperor the Brief was retracted by the decree *Non Indecens Videtus* the following year, on June 19, 1538.[43] Since Paul was certainly pressured by Charles, it was likely felt that more harm than good was being done by this direct contradiction of a royal edict of the King of Spain. It should be noted that Paul was not giving approbation to any unjust forms of slavery by this action of revocation. While Charles may have thought that the Pope had annulled both *Pastorale* and *Sublimis*, this was not the case.[44]

---

[43] Parish, *Las Casas en Mexico*, 313-314.

[44] One may draw the wrong conclusion about what was revoked by *Non Indecens* from John Tracy Ellis's commentary on Paul III's *Sublimis Deus*: "As a consequence, the Pope issued another bull on June 19, 1538, which revoked *all previous papal briefs and bulls* that might prejudice the power of Charles V in his colonial empire" [emphasis added]. *Documents*, I, 7.

Lewis Hanke in 1937 noted, "Whether the Pope promised Charles that he would revoke the bulls as well as the brief remains for future historians to discover" (*Harvard Theological Review*, XXX, 91). At the same time, Hanke's remarks anticipated the later conclusions of Parish, Gutierrez and others when he stated that, "At first sight this brief would not seem to refer to the bulls *Sublimis Deus* and *Veritas Ipsa* [Hanke believes them to be two separate documents], for only 'letters in the form of a brief' (*in forma brevis litteras*) are mentioned... the bulls *Sublimis Deus* and *Veritas Ipsa* are not mentioned in the brief of revocation" (*Review*, XXX, 89).

Gutierrez states: "According to the king of Spain, then, *Sublimis Deus*, and not only the letter to Tavera [*Pastorale Officium*], has been annulled by the brief *Non Indecens*... Everything indicates that this is what he [Charles V] requested and, mistakenly, thought he obtained. There is every indication, then, that only the brief *Pastorale Officium* has been abrogated" (Gutierrez, *Las Casas*, 310). See also: Parish, *Las Casas en Mexico*, Appendices, No. 41.

Sublimis Deus does not make mention of Charles V in any way, but rather, as stated above, was intended to be the primary and universal teaching document that would give doctrinal basis to *Pastorale Officium* and other works. In order to maintain the cooperation of the Spanish civil authorities in improving the spiritual and temporal welfare of the Indians, it was felt that the revocation of the penalties of *Pastorale* was needed. Its teaching — as distinguished from its penalties — was enshrined in the Bull *Sublimis Deus*, written to the entire Christian world. Indeed the value of *Pastorale* itself would be maintained by several later popes.[45]

Altitudo Divini Consilii, June 1, 1537

Another work of Paul III that deserves mention is *Altitudo Divini Consilii*. This document was addressed to the Bishops of the Indies, and dealt with the religious preparation of the Indians for reception of the Sacraments. They were from that point onward to be treated and prepared for Christian initiation according to the same norms that the Church applied to, say, European converts.[46] This was of course because they were rational, "true men," with the same freedom and humanity. *Altitudo Divini Consilii* is thus applying the teachings on the freedom and humanity of the Indians contained in *Sublimis Deus* and *Pastorale Officium* to the requirements for reception into the faith.

Consistent with his teachings in *Sublimis* and *Pastorale* against the plundering by the slave makers of what rightfully belongs to the Indians, Paul issued the Motu Proprio *Cupientes Judaeos* on March 21, 1542. This instruction was given in order to

---

[45] Interestingly, both the Latin of *Denzinger* (DS 1495) and the newest German edition, *Denzinger-Huenermann*, cite the teaching of *Pastorale Officium*. Both texts incorrectly state that *Veritas* was repeating the penalty of excommunication contained in *Pastorale*, but neither this draft version nor *Sublimis Deus* itself mention penalties.

[46] Gutierrez, *Las Casas*, 307-308.

protect the rights of the Indians who had recently entered, or were preparing to receive, the Faith. Out of fear that they would lose their property to the Christians or others, many of these converts were going back on their intention to accept the faith. Paul therefore declares that it is forbidden for anyone to deprive these people of their property, even for parents to deprive their children, under the penalty of excommunication.[47]

Of the three documents of Paul III we have just considered, Parish writes:

> In brief: these three apostolic letters not only proclaimed the universal human rights and rationality and liberty of the Indians, but also ordered the missionaries to respect these principles which were to be defended against the Spaniards with the most severe sanctions.[48]

> The encyclical *Sublimis Deus* and the other two decrees were in reality epoch making. The promulgation of these apostolic letters literally marked the true beginning of international law in the modern world: the first intercontinental proclamation of the rights inherent in all men and the liberty of nations.[49]

The latter statement is particularly impressive, a great tribute to both Paul III and the teaching office he held. Missionaries, in particular Las Casas, influenced the writing of, and subsequently used, *Sublimis Deus* in their efforts to bring an end to the unjust enslavement of the Indians by the Spanish.[50] One of the premier theologians of the day, Francis de Vitoria, himself influenced by *Sublimis*,

---

[47] Hernaez, *Coleccion*, I, 97-99. The *Cupientes* is explicitly renewed by Clement XI in his Motu Proprio *Propagandae per Universum Terrarum* of March 11, 1704 (*Coleccion*, I, 100).

[48] Parish, *Las Casas en Mexico*, 19.

[49] *Ibid.*, 18.

[50] Parish states that Las Casas's work *De Unico Modo* (*The Only Way*) had a substantial influence on the teaching of *Sublimis Deus*: "[*The Only Way*] was the basis, point by point, of the great papal encyclical *Sublimis Deus*, proclaiming the rationality and liberty of the Indians and the peaceful way to convert them" (Las Casas, *The Only Way*, ed. by Parish, 4).

wrote and taught extensively in defense of the Indians in his works which many consider the beginning of international law. He made a respectable effort to apply *Sublimis Deus* to his writings just two years after the Bull was issued. Some of the relevant opinions in his *First Relectio, 'De Indis'*, include: the Indians are not irrational, and are true owners of their possessions; they are not, as Aristotle suggested some men might be, "slaves by nature"; the Pope has no jurisdiction over non-Christians, and a failure to accept the authority of the Pope is not a just cause for war; the right to claim new lands only applies if they are uninhabited; forcing the Indians to accept the faith is impossible, and their refusal of Christianity is not a just cause for waging war on them; the decision of the Indians to accept the dominion of the Spaniards must be truly free, and not vitiated by other factors such as force, fear or ignorance.[51]

It must be noted, however, that Vitoria also taught that there were several titles by which Spain might acquire dominion over the Indians, even using war and enslavement as a last resort: the right of the Spaniards to travel in international waters, and to be treated fairly by foreigners as long as they come in peace; the right to free trade and to seek out supplies of commonly held natural resources; the right to defend their colonists and missionaries; the right to preach the Gospel, though *a refusal to accept* that Gospel is *not* a just cause for war; the obligation in justice and charity to prevent the practice of cannibalism or ritual human sacrifice.[52] Vitoria's opinions should be taken as a very enlightened *first* attempt to articulate the rights of the non-Europeans in international law, rather than as a perfect end. Even while operating under pressure from the Spanish government, Vitoria managed to produce a

---

[51] Eppstein, *Catholic Law*, 432-443. On this last point, Vitoria was teaching no more than what had previously been taught by Alexander VI's Bull *Ineffabilis et Summi Patris* (see Alexander VI, above).

[52] *Ibid.*, 443-456. For example, the native peoples of Mexico practiced human sacrifice of slaves and prisoners of war, beginning around 2500 BC. This increased substantially after 1430 AD, was carried on well into the next century, and even included the sacrificial offering of children. See Thomas, *Conquest*, esp. 24-27.

respectable, though flawed, application of the magisterial teachings. Clearly, his intention was to be a defender of the rights of the Indians, and his overall success and influence in this regard was to secure his place in history as just such a man.[53]

It has been said by several authors that in a Motu Proprio issued in Rome on November 8, 1548, Paul III approved of slavery in Rome. Little effort is made by such authors to understand the true meaning of the document.[54] When one looks at the historical facts surrounding the issuance of this letter, it becomes obvious that slavery in general was not sanctioned, but rather that only those held as prisoners of war were for a time allowed to be held in Rome:

> That this document was truly treating of prisoners taken in war, according to the custom of the time, and not treating of

---

[53] Maxwell gives slight treatment to the writings of Vitoria, placing him in the same section as those who wished to defend the Spanish conquerors rather than the Indians; Vitoria is clearly in a different league than men such as Palacios Rubios or Sepulveda, who both attempted to justify the Spanish war on the Indians through the "slaves by nature" theory proposed by Aristotle. Sepulveda is also reported to have made reference to a papal decree authorizing war on the Indians. He must have made the same fallacious jump as Maxwell does, from the Brief *Romanus Pontifex* of Nicholas V to the Bull *Inter Caetera* of Alexander VI (*Slavery*, 62, 80, and Alexander VI, above).

Noonan, in his attempt to prove that slavery is an area where the Church has changed its moral teaching, gives no reference to Vitoria at all. He is, however, willing to cite Vitoria's rival, Cardinal Juan De Lugo: "The eminent Jesuit moralist Cardinal Juan De Lugo was in harmony with the moralist tradition when he found slavery 'beyond the intention of nature,' but 'introduced to prevent greater evils'" ("Development in Moral Doctrine," *Theological Studies*, 666). To fail to cite Vitoria, another major theologian of the sixteenth century (who was even invited to the Council of Trent), especially on the issue of slavery, is hardly an even-handed approach.

[54] Of the Motu Proprio, John T. Noonan states that "Paul III praised the benevolent effects of slavery on agriculture while approving the traffic in slaves in Rome." "Development," *Theological Studies* 54, 666.

Maxwell also refers to this letter of Paul III, dating it November 9th instead of November 8th: "[Paul III]... declared the lawfulness of slave-trading and slave-holding, including the holding of Christian slaves, in Rome" (*Slavery*, 75).

The impression one may get from reading Maxwell's quotation of this letter — cited as it is without any attempt to interpret its true meaning — and from that of Noonan, is that Paul somehow gave approval to all slavery in Rome. This is an illogical interpretation that does not include the distinction between legal servitude and unjust slavery. In light of Paul's strong teachings issued in 1537 against unjust enslavement of people in the New World, this latter document should be understood as applying only to those held in Italy under the various legal titles to servitude.

free men who by fraud or violence were deprived of their liberty and reduced to slavery, is a fact about which there can be no doubt whatsoever.[55]

---

[55] "*Che poi si trattasse veramente di prigionieri fatti in guerra, secondo il diritto allora vigente, e non già di uomini liberi, per frode o per violenza privati della loro libertà e ridotti a servitù, è un fatto, sul quale non cade dubbio alcuno,*" Salvatore M. Brandi, S.J., *Il Papato E La Schiavitù* (Rome: Civiltà Cattolica, 1903), 29. This work is a fuller presentation, both in text and footnote citations, than the version that appeared in *La Civiltà Cattolica* X (1903), 545-561, 677-694.

Salvatore Brandi's work proves that some things change very little. At the turn of the century the Church faced criticism of its teaching on slavery. In 1903 Brandi responded to such criticism as it appeared in a Roman newspaper, *The Tribune*. The conclusion of Brandi's study is cited above. The essential points of his study can be summarized as follows:

First of all, Brandi explains what kind of servitude is permitted in Rome by Pope Paul III, and what the conditions surrounding Paul's decree were. Brandi writes:

"When Pope Paul III, in 1534, ascended the pontifical throne, he found that already for a long time every sort of slavery, properly speaking, had been abolished in Rome, and that, beyond that, there was even forbidden that type of servitude, according to just title, that was permitted by other rulers in their countries. This fact did not do away with the occurrence that male and female slaves from other places would flee to Rome and end up being introduced furtively into Roman families and there held illegally and even against their will, being prevented from having recourse to the Conservatori of Rome to reclaim their liberty under the pretext that the power of granting the same no longer existed in the Roman Senate, or at least was doubtfully existent. Paul III, knowing this, with solicitude wanted to remedy this abuse. And so he directed a Motu Proprio, dated June 28, 1535 to the Conservatori..." (pp. 23-34).

The Conservatori were the group of Roman magistrates who had the power to free the escaped prisoners of war. In his Motu Proprio, Paul III ratified this power, and followed the Motu Proprio with a Letter on May 29, 1537 that clearly restated Paul III's abhorrence of slavery. This Letter was, of course, *Pastorale Officium* (although Brandi mistakenly believed it to be *Veritas Ipsa*).

Paul III's teaching was followed with reluctance on the part of the Romans, and even by the Conservatori. In November 1544, the Roman Senate asked Paul to reconsider his decree. He refused, and his Motu Proprio remained in effect until April 1548. Then the Conservatori again petitioned him by almost unanimous vote (35 out of 39) to reconsider. Because of the war with the Turks, the number of prisoners of war in Rome had increased markedly. These prisoners were held, according to the just title theory of the times, as slaves. The number who had fled to Rome and obtained their freedom was so great that to provide for them was a great burden on the city government. Furthermore, the economy of Rome had grown accustomed to the labor of such prsioners, although this was against the decree of the Pope. (The papal historian Ludwig von Pastor makes it clear that this illicit activity was against the will of Paul III. He wrote: "Even in Rome the Pope was unable at once to carry out effectually his efforts against slavery, and the position of *captive unbelievers* in Italy still continued to be one of bondage" [emphasis added]. Cf. Pastor, *The History of the Popes*, ed. by Ralph Francis Kerr [St. Louis: B. Herder, 1912]).

Gregory XIV: *Cum Sicuti,* April 18, 1591

Niccolo Sfondrati was born near Milan on February 11, 1535. His pious life and commitment to reforming the Church were both greatly influenced by his friendship with the future saint, Charles Borromeo, and by his devotion to St. Philip Neri and the Oratory. Working throughout his life for reform, he attended the final session of the Council of Trent, and then implemented those reforms in his own diocese of Cremona. After being elected Pope on December 5, 1990, Gregory XIV was to be hindered in his efforts to effect change by a weak constitution, lack of political experience, and a short pontificate that ended less than a year later, on October 16, 1591.[56]

The Bull *Cum Sicuti* was issued by Gregory on April 18, 1591 to the Bishop of Manila in the Philippines. The Spaniards had used force against the Indians, unjustly subduing them under the pretext of spreading the faith. Gregory notes that the natives were in fact hostile, but that much harm has been done to them by their conquerors:

> ... when the Philippines were first converted, the Indians were very fierce and many took up arms against them because of the great danger to their own lives. Much harm was done to the Indians in such a conflict. Now... there are many who

---

Finally, after being pressured by the Conservatori for fourteen years, Paul III wrote the Motu Proprio of November 8, 1548. It allowed servitude according to the just titles in Rome, primarily for captives of war.

When Pius V became Pope he discovered that Paul's concession of November 1548 (published in January 1549) was being interpreted in such a way that all prisoners taken from the Turks were being treated as slaves, even when such were baptized Christians who had previously been enslaved by the Turks. The taking into slavery of Christians who had been freed from the Turkish galleys was forbidden, and Pius V repeated this, saying that Paul III's document was not to be understood as permitting the same. The document of Pius V is entitled *Licet Omnibus Notissimum* of 1570. This was followed by his Motu Proprio, *Postquam Nuper* of 1571, forbidding even the selling of slave prisoners of war during the actual war. He mandated that they be treated well, and close account kept of them, thus anticipating by a few centuries the work of the Geneva Conventions.

[56] Kelly, *Popes,* 273-274.

realize that the deprivation of the Indians was wrong, and who wish to make restitution...[57]

Restitution is to be made by the Spaniards, either immediately or when their means allow, to those Indians who are known to have been wronged. If it is not known exactly which Indians were harmed, a Congregation of the bishop and other local Church leaders should be called. There a settlement should be arranged that gives preference to all of the Indians in need, thereby putting the Christian faith in a better light and aiding in the cause of salvation of souls.

Gregory issued *Cum Sicuti* not only to settle matters of conscience, but also to lend Church support to the antislavery decree of Philip II:

> Furthermore, since, as we have learned, Philip the Catholic King of Spain, our beloved son in Christ, has forbidden that any Spaniard in those Philippine Islands dare to make, have or retain slaves (*mancipia sive servos... facere vel habere seu retinere audeant*), whether by just or unjust war, or through sale or any other title or pretext among the many frauds accustomed to be committed there, and that some do in fact still detain slaves against that edict and mandate of King Philip, We — in order that the Indians may come to or return to Christian doctrine and their own homes and possessions freely and securely and without any fear of servitude, as befits what is in harmony with reason and justice — decree in virtue of holy obedience and under penalty of excommunication that if, at the publication of these letters, anyone have or detain such Indians slaves they must give up all craft and deceit, set the slaves completely free and in the future neither make nor retain slaves in any way (*nec servos ullo modo faciant aut retineant*), according to the edict and mandate of said King Philip.[58]

---

[57] See Appendix B, No. 5.
[58] *Ibid.*, 108.

Note that Gregory reiterates the penalty of excommunication of *Pastorale Officium*. The Spanish civil authorities are once again willing to support such a sanction as a disciplinary means of enforcing the consistent magisterial teaching. Gregory additionally notes and gives approval to Philip's mandate against taking slaves "whether by just or unjust war" because of the obvious abuse that has occurred in the Philippines. The unjust war waged on the Filipinos was done under the false pretext that such an action was somehow justified because of the hostility of the Indians towards accepting the faith. This abuse the King of Spain is now willing to help prevent from happening again. Also, the operative principles of the Bull are stated to be "what is in harmony with reason and justice." It is only reasonable and in accord with the virtue of justice that those people who have been unjustly held as slaves be set free, have their possessions returned to them and that restitution be made for the wrongs committed.

THE THIRD HUNDRED YEARS
(1639-1740)

Urban VIII: *Commissum Nobis*, April 22, 1639

Maffeo Barberini was born in Florence in 1568, elected to head the Church on August 6, 1623, and reigned until July 29, 1644. As Urban VIII, he centralized Church authority in himself rather than rely on the help of his cardinals. He spent profusely on his nepotist concerns and on beautifying Rome, consecrating the new St. Peter's Basilica in 1626. He helped revise the breviary and the procedure for canonizing saints, and was active in supporting missionary efforts. The second condemnation of Galileo occurred under his tenure, and in an attempt to prevent the conception of that

most dismal of heresies fathered by Cornelius Jansen, Urban censured his work, *Augustinus*, in 1642.[59]

We begin now to consider a series of papal bulls which have in common the fact that they make reference to the teachings of their predecessors. This was done in order to lend historical proof to the consistency of the Church's teaching against unjust enslavement. The first of these bulls is *Commissum Nobis*,[60] issued on April 22, 1639 to the Collector General of debts for the Apostolic Camera in Portugal. It was written at the request of the procurator of the Province of Paraguay, Father Francisco Diartano, S.J., and also to lend ecclesiastical support to a 1626 Royal Edict of King Philip IV opposing enslavement of the Indians.[61] First, Urban indicates that the office of the Pope obliges him to exercise concern for the salvation of all people:

> The ministry of the highest apostolic office, entrusted to us by the Lord, demands that the salvation of no one be outside our concern, not only the salvation of the Christian faithful but also the salvation of those who still exist outside the bosom of the Church in the darkness of native superstition.[62]

---

[59] Kelly, *Popes*, 280-281.

[60] The commentary of Hernaez states that Fr. Antonio Ruiz de Montoya, missionary and Procurator of Paraguay, refers to a 1605 prohibition of Clement VIII, the original text of which has not been discovered. On this same work of Clement, a certain Solorzano, in Book 2, Chapter 5 of his *Politica Indiana*, says that "The same [teaching] as Paul III — in his Brief of 1537 — seems to have been agreed with and mandated by Clement VIII" (Hernaez, *Coleccion*, I, 109).

[61] Hernaez, *Coleccion*, I, 110-111. Hernaez notes here that the Holy Office had tried previously to stop the abuses against the Indians in 1634.

Maxwell states that not only Urban VIII, but also Paul III, Gregory XIV, and Benedict XIV (forthcoming) issued their antislavery bulls "for this same reason of preserving harmony between the civil and ecclesiastical courts…" (*Slavery*, 72). However, the fact that these bulls were issued at different times after the appearance of various Royal edicts indicates the desire of the Church to support the civil authorities in defense of the Indians, and not merely to maintain legal continuity with them. Furthermore, Maxwell fails to note that the Spanish Kings were acting on a Catholic community and according to the teaching of the Magisterium.

[62] See Appendix B, No. 6.

The Third Hundred Years

He then considers the antislavery efforts of Pope Paul III:

> At another time our predecessor Paul III desired to take measures in respect to the condition of the Indians of the West and South who were being reduced to slavery (*in servitutem redigi*), deprived of their property, and for that reason kept from embracing faith in Christ: he forbade and commanded to be forbidden that said Indians be in any way reduced to slavery (*Indos quomodolibet in servitutem redigere*), or despoiled of their property as well as other things clearly contained in a similar Brief of May 29, 1537 of the same Paul III. He decreed for each and every individual of any dignity, state, condition, or degree who violated his decree the incurring of the penalty of excommunication, *latae sententiae*.[63]

Urban seems first to be referring to the teachings against enslaving and plundering the Indians that are contained in *Sublimis Deus*. The "similar brief" of May 29, 1537 would of course be *Pastorale Officium*, of which both the teaching and the penalty of excommunication are noted. This indicates that Urban saw both of Paul's works as teaching the same thing, and also that he apparently considered the excommunications of *Pastorale* still in effect.

Noting that the same injustices existed in his time in the Provinces of Paraguay, Brazil, and Rio de la Plata (Argentina), as well as other parts of South America, Urban then writes:

> We ourselves, following the footsteps of Paul our Predecessor and wishing to repress the efforts of impious men who should induce said Indians to accept faith in Christ by all the means of Christian charity and gentleness but who deter them from it by their inhuman acts, entrust to you the duty and command you by these present letters that, either by yourself or through another or through others that you severely prohibit anyone from reducing to slavery (*in servitutem redigere*), selling, buying exchanging, giving away, separating from wives and children, despoiling of their property, taking away

---
[63] See Appendix B, No. 6.

> to other places, depriving of liberty in any way and keeping in servitude said Indians... This injunction applies to each and every person, both secular and ecclesiastic... Any of these contravening this decree incur, by that fact, the penalty of excommunication *latae sententiae*...[64]

The desire of Urban VIII to teach exactly what Paul III taught is very apparent, from the statement that he is "following in the footsteps of Paul," to the use of the same phrase as that of Paul — "reducing to slavery" (*in servitutem redigere*) — to his issuing of the same penalty of excommunication *latae sententiae*, absolution of which is reserved to the Roman Pontiff alone. Thus the teachings of not only *Sublimis Deus*, but also those of *Pastorale Officium* together with its penalties, are affirmed and reiterated a century later.

Innocent XI: *Response of the Congregation of the Holy Office, No. 230,* March 20, 1686

Benedetto Odescalchi was born in Como, Italy on May 19, 1611, and served as a legal aid for Urban VIII. Both pious and an effective administrator, Innocent gave much of his income as the Cardinal-Bishop of Novara to the poor, and would accept the papal office when elected on September 21, 1676 only after his program of Church reform was adopted. He restored the troubled finances of the Vatican, worked for the moral reform of the clergy and religious, and called for more evangelizing and catechizing, especially frequent reception of Communion. His most noted accomplishment was to turn back the advancement of the Turks into Europe. Innocent XI was declared "blessed" by Pius XII on October 7, 1956, and his feast day is commemorated on August 12th (d. 1689).[65]

---

[64] *Ibid.*, No. 6.
[65] Kelly, *Popes*, 287-288.

Beginning around the middle of the sixteenth century, the need for a cheap source of human labor both in Europe and in the New World led to the shameless European enslavement of the people of Africa. As in the Americas, the Europeans did not themselves begin the practice of enslaving the Africans. They did, however, expand tremendously what had been begun in Africa under Arab and Moslem auspices from about the 11th century.[66] In the Western Hemisphere, the Indian population of unjustly held slaves in Central and South America was quickly diminishing, and the colonization of North America had already begun. The same fallacious excuses were to be proposed in Africa as in the New World in a superficial attempt to gain moral approval of what was clearly the unjust enslavement of millions. Since most Africans were non-Christian, many taught, as had been the case in the New World, that war could be waged on these "enemies of Christianity," especially those who were Muslims.[67] This argument of course fails because there was no real warfare occurring between the Europeans and the Africans who were being enslaved.

The Congregation of the Holy Office was established in 1542 as the final court of appeals for trials of heresy. As an organ of each papal administration, its role was gradually expanded to address other issues expressly dealing with questions concerning the faith. In 1965 the title was changed to The Congregation for the Doctrine of the Faith.

During the pontificate of Innocent XI, on March 20, 1686, several questions were asked of the Holy Office concerning the morality of enslaving the natives of Africa. The first three questions of *Instruction Number 230* concern the action of taking the Africans as slaves:

It is asked:
1. Whether it is permitted to capture by force or deceit Blacks (*nigros*) or other natives (*sylvestres*) who have harmed no one.

---

[66] *The New Catholic Encyclopedia*, "Slavery (History of)," by C. Verlinden, 286-287.
[67] Gutierrez, *Las Casas*, 319-321.

2. Whether it is permitted to buy, sell or make other contracts in their respect Blacks or other natives who have harmed no one and been made captives by force or deceit.
3. Whether it is permitted to buy Blacks or other natives, unjustly captured and who are now mixed among other salable goods.

Response:
To numbers 1, 2, 3: it is not permitted.[68]

From the negative response given to the first proposition, it is clear that the capture of black people for the purpose of enslavement is condemned. The fact that these people "have harmed no one" shows that they are neither considered to be the enemies of Christianity, nor engaged in war with their enslavers. Attempts to enslave the black people under the cloaking of a religious war is not legitimate. The second proposition develops further the teaching of the first by extending the condemnation of enslavement to cover also the trade in black slaves. Lastly, the *Instruction* in the third proposition does not accept the argument that slave marketing could be justified by the trading practices of the time.

The second three questions of *Instruction 230* address the obligations of those who own or wish to own slaves:

It is asked:
4. Whether buyers of Blacks and other natives are not obliged to inquire about their title of servitude, viz. whether they have justly or unjustly been enslaved [*sintne iuste vel iniuste*], even when they know that very many of them have been unjustly captured.
5. Whether the possessors of Blacks and other natives who have harmed no one and been captured by force or deceit, are not obliged to set them free.
6. Whether the captors, buyers and possessors of Blacks and

---
[68] See Appendix C, No. 1.

other natives who have harmed no one and who have been captured by force or deceit are not obliged to make compensation to them.

Response:

To numbers 4, 5, and 6: they are obliged.[69]

The fourth proposition is perhaps the most interesting of the series. What is required of one who is seeking to purchase slaves is that he must discover the nature of the title under which those slaves are held. This of course goes back to the distinction made in the First Chapter between the just and unjust titles to servitude. If the purchaser discovers that those in servitude are held as criminals or as captives of a just war, then he may obtain them, keeping in mind his obligation to treat them according to the precepts of justice and charity. If, however, he learns that the slaves are held unjustly as innocent people who have been forcibly captured, then he may not acquire them. The final words of the fourth proposition, "even when they know that very many of them have been unjustly captured," indicates that the reality of the situation in Africa was such that few, if any, of the people taken and sold as slaves were in fact justly held. We will see this important distinction being made again in future Holy Office instructions.

The fifth proposition requires that all black people and other residents who have been captured and enslaved be restored to freedom. Lastly, the sixth proposition demands that proper compensation be made for the injustices the Africans have suffered from those who have unjustly taken, bought or currently possess these people as slaves. This is in addition to the restoration of liberty demanded by the fifth proposition.

The propositions considered in *Instruction 230*, presented and responded to in that concise format that was typical even earlier in our own century of the Congregation for the Doctrine of the Faith, are important because they show that the Magisterium did not fail

---
[69] *Ibid.*, No. 1.

to address early on the issue of slavery amongst the African people. It may *appear* that the Magisterium only belatedly addressed the issue of the black African slavery that began about 1550. However, the actual nature of the servitude practiced in Africa was unclear for some time, due to the lack of colonies there. Furthermore, the Magisterium already had a clear teaching against such unjust slavery two and a half centuries before this *Instruction*, beginning in 1435 with the issuance of *Sicut Dudum* on behalf of the black peoples of the Canary Islands. This teaching was readily known by the Europeans, and should have been applied by them to the Africans. Also, as noted earlier, Paul III explicitly taught in *Sublimis Deus* that "all other peoples... who shall hereafter come to the knowledge of Christians are not to have been deprived nor be deprived of their liberty..."[70]

THE LAST ONE HUNDRED AND FIFTY YEARS
(1741-1890)

Benedict XIV: *Immensa Pastorum*, December 20, 1741

Prospero Lorenzo Lambertini was born March 31, 1675 in Bologna. After an education in theology and law, he advanced quickly, serving as advisor to Benedict XIII. His namesake predecessor in turn appointed him a cardinal in 1728, and as a dark horse at the 1740 conclave was selected Pope as a compromise. Politi-

---

[70] Of the efforts of the Popes we are considering, Maxwell states that "It is noticeable that not one of this series of Papal Briefs makes any reference to the enslavement of the Negroes in West Africa nor to the transatlantic trade in Negro slaves. It was not until the nineteenth century... that this omission was rectified." (*Slavery*, 73). Maxwell draws this wrong conclusion because he does not realize that the Holy Office is a true organ of the Pope and the Magisterium, and because he does not recognize the extent of Paul III's teaching.

cally, Benedict was both adept and realistic. He improved relations with several countries through the signing of concordats, while at home reforming the papal states finances. He also pressed for reform of the episcopacy, seminaries, and the liturgical calendar, as well as established academies for a wide range of scholarly pursuits. Benedict's amiable personality, moderate views, administrative effectiveness and holiness of life gained him the approval of many. Aware of the cronyism and nepotism of previous pontiffs, Horace Walpole described Benedict as "a priest without insolence or interest, a prince without favorites, a pope without nephews."[71]

Benedict XIV continues the tradition of his predecessors by issuing *Immensa Pastorum* to the Bishops of Brazil and all other regions under the dominion of King John of Portugal on December 20, 1741. Benedict begins by stating that it is because of the charity Our Lord Jesus Christ exercised in redeeming all people that he, Christ's representative on earth, is called "to lay down [his] life not only for Christ's faithful, but also for all men whatsoever."[72] He then provides a general recollection of the efforts of the Church to prevent slavery:

> We have received written notice, not without most grave sorrow to our fatherly soul, that, after so much advice of Apostolic providence given by our Predecessors the Roman Pontiffs, after the publication of Constitutions, saying that help, aid, and protection should be given to those who lack faith, and that neither injuries, nor the scourge, nor chains, nor servitude, nor death should be inflicted on them, and all this under the gravest penalties and censures of the Church...[73]

During Benedict's pontificate, some Christians continued to enslave the Indian people in and around Brazil (continued from above):

---

[71] Kelly, *Popes*, 297-298.
[72] See Appendix B, No. 7.
[73] *Ibid.*, No. 7.

> ... there are still found, especially in the regions of Brazil, members of the True Faith who... presume to deal with the unfortunate Indians who dwell in the harsh mountain regions of the same Brazil, whether north or south or in other deserted regions — not only those who lack the Faith, but even those cleansed by the washing of regeneration [baptism] — by reducing them to slavery (*redigere servitutem*), or selling them to others as if they were property (*aut veluti mancipia aliis vendere*), or depriving them of their goods, or dealing with them inhumanly, so that they are strongly turned from embracing faith in Christ and are greatly confirmed in a hatred for it...[74]

After exhorting his bishops to provide assistance to the Indians, meaning both material help and the gift of the Faith, Benedict recalls two important efforts of his predecessors:

> Furthermore, we, by Apostolic authority, and holding to the same course, renew and confirm the Apostolic Letters in the form of a Brief written by our Predecessor Pope Paul III to John of Tavera, then Cardinal of the Holy Roman Church and Archbishop of Toledo on May 28, 1537,[75] and by our Predecessor Urban VIII to the then Collector-General of Debts of the Apostolic Camera in Portugal on April 22, 1639.[76]

In case anyone believed that the teaching in *Pastorale Officium* was somehow no longer in force, Benedict renewed and confirmed Paul III's two-century-old Brief against slavery. Also confirmed and renewed is *Commisum Nobis* of Urban VIII, issued a century earlier to the same territories as Benedict's *Immensa Pastorum*.

The Pope then tells how the Indians are to be treated, and who is obliged to follow the decree:

---

[74] *Ibid.*, No. 7.
[75] Both the *Bullarium* of Benedict XIV (I, 101), and the *Coleccion* (I, 113) incorrectly record the date of *Pastorale Officium* as May 28th instead of May 29th.
[76] See Appendix B, No. 7.

> Following in the footsteps of the same Paul and Urban our Predecessors... We command... that you efficaciously assist said Indians, and let it be known that each and every person, both secular and ecclesiastic of whatever status, sex, grade, condition and dignity, even those worthy of special note and dignity, of any Order, Congregation, Society (even the Society of Jesus), Religion, Mendicant and non-Mendicant, monks, Regulars, as well as the Military Brotherhood, even the Hospitalers of St. John of Jerusalem, who contravenes these edicts will incur, *eo ipso*, excommunication *latae sententiae*. From this excommunication they can be absolved only by us or by the Roman Pontiff then existing...[77]

Benedict reiterates his call to give the Indians temporal and spiritual assistance, and then tells who must abide by his instructions. It is interesting that first Urban, and then Benedict, were at pains to include all of the members of the clergy and religious orders in their injunctions. At least for the first century (1435-1537), from Eugene IV to Paul III, the papal decrees seemed to be directed primarily at civil and military authorities. Eugene IV's *Sicut Dudum* was issued in 1435 for the following:

> ... one and all, temporal princes, lords, captains, armed men, barons, soldiers, nobles, communities, and all others of every kind among the Christian faithful of whatever state, grade or condition ...[78]

Likewise, Paul III's 1537 Brief *Pastorale Officium* was directed towards "anyone of whatever dignity, state, condition or grade."[79] However, when we arrive a century later at Urban VIII's *Commissum Nobis*, it is rather the clergy and religious of the Church who are targeted specifically:

> This injunction applies to each and every person, both secular and ecclesiastic, of whatever state, sex degree, condition

---
[77] *Ibid.*, No. 7.
[78] *Ibid.*, No. 1.

and dignity, even those worthy of special recognition and mention, and to those belonging to any order, congregation, society, religious body, institute, mendicants and non-mendicants, as well as monks and regular clergy.[80]

The same can be said of Benedict XIV's 1741 Bull, given above, which even lists particular religious orders by name. The development here of the teaching is readily apparent, and thus leads to the conclusion that members of the clergy and religious orders were likely a growing part of the slavery problem in and around Brazil during the two centuries from Paul III to Benedict XIV. Most likely, many priests and religious were refusing to accept and teach what was contained in the antislavery documents of the Papal Magisterium.

Lastly, Benedict lists the unjust actions that are condemned and result in the penalty of excommunication:

> Those incur this penalty who reduce said Indians to slavery (*praedictos Indos in servitutem redigere*), sell them, buy them, exchange them or give them away, separate them from their wives and children, despoil them of their property and goods, lead or transmit them to other places, or in any manner deprive them of liberty to retain them in servitude; as well as those who offer counsel, aid or favor those who do such things; We declare that anyone who contradicts or rebels against these things or does not agree with you in respect to said matters falls under penalty of this excommunication, as well as under any other ecclesiastical censures and penalties and other opportune remedies ...[81]

---

[79] *Ibid.*, No. 4.

[80] *Ibid.*, No. 6

[81] *Ibid.*, No. 7. Hernaez states in his commentary: "It should be noted regarding the excommunication, that it is suppressed by the Bull *Apostolicae Sedis*, October 12, 1869. Nevertheless the prohibition of the pontiff always remains" (*Coleccion*, I, 114). The same is noted of *Commisum Nobis* and *Pastorale Officium* (*Coleccion*, I, 111, 102). *Apostolicae Sedis* provided a general revision of many canonical censures by Pope Pius IX. The excommunications for violations of the papal bulls against slavery were abrogated because it was felt that they were no longer needed (See *Acta Pius IX*,

The latter half of this paragraph indicates that there was indeed a problem with people who gave counsel or support to the actions of the slave makers, or who in other ways contradicted and disagreed with the Church's teaching against slavery.

The antislavery attitude of the popes perdured from Benedict XIV until the time of Gregory XVI. We can see this attitude reflected in the various efforts of Pius VII, whose pontificate lasted from 1800 to 1823. In his 1839 Bull *In Supremo*, Gregory XVI noted the following of the efforts made by Pius on behalf of the enslaved:

> In our time Pius VII, moved by the same religious and charitable spirit as his Predecessors, dutifully used his good offices with those in power to end completely the slave trade at least among Christians.[82]

However, since those efforts — noting especially the 1814-1815 Congress of Vienna — produced no formal Magisterial document, they are not of direct concern here.[83]

5:55-72). It is interesting that Hernaez mentions *Pastorale Officium*, which had been revoked by the decree *Non Indecens Videtus*. It appears that Hernaez for all practical purposes, like many of the successors of Paul III, viewed *Pastorale*, with its excommunications, as in effect long after the 1538 revocation.

[82] See Appendix B, No. 8.

[83] "There exist, in the Vatican Archives, the Briefs on slavery addressed by the Pontiff [Pius VII] to the Sovereigns of France, Spain and Portugal. To end the traffic in Blacks, the Pope in 1814 associated himself with the Powers in the antislavery deliberations of the Congress of Vienna." Brandi, *La Schiavitù*, 17. Cited from Artaud De Montor, *Histoire de la vie et du Pontificat du Pape Pie VII*, Paris, 1836.

The antislavery efforts of Pius VII and Cardinal Consalvi are also mentioned in an article entitled, "Santa Sede e L'Inghilterra Nell'Anno 1814," found in *La Civiltà Cattolica* VII (1902), pp. 157-179. The relevant material is summarized below.

The article deals with the visit to London in July of 1814 of Cardinal Consalvi, the papal Secretary of State. This was the eve of the Congress of Vienna, which had been called to bring peace to Europe at the end of the Napoleonic wars. In London, Consalvi had a long interview with Lord Castlereagh, the Prime Minister of England. This was the highest contact of the Holy See and England since the Reformation. What is important in this article is that it contains the text of Consalvi's letter of July 5, 1814 from London to Cardinal Pacca in Rome, the letter giving details of the interview with Lord Castlereagh. The text of the letter is found on pages 165 to 176. In the letter, Consalvi notes how Castlereagh initiated the conversation regarding the slave trade,

Gregory XVI: *In Supremo,* December 3, 1839

Bartolomeo Alberto Cappellari was born in Venice on September 18, 1765. After entering the monastic life and being ordained in 1787, he taught science and philosophy, wrote in defense of papal infallibility and as a cardinal served effectively as Prefect of the Missions. After being elected the Successor of Peter on February 2, 1831, he worked to oppose modern ideas he saw as rooted in indifferentism and other intellectual systems. He also sought to obtain an independent Church, and opposed the revolutions that led to anticlerical governments. His continued concern for a revival of the missions led to the creation of seventy new dioceses and vicariates and the appointment of two hundred missionary bishops throughout the world.[84]

The 1839 Constitution *In Supremo* of Gregory XVI continued the antislavery teaching of his predecessors, and was in the same manner not accepted by many of those bishops, priests and

---

saying that England wanted the Pope's help at the Congress of Vienna to have the trade outlawed. Consalvi admits that he was very much impressed that, with all the concerns Castlereagh had at that time, he should give such prominence to this issue:
"The fact is that the abolition of this inhuman commerce has been taken so much to the heart of this nation that the voices of humanity and of justice have silenced the voices of self-interest, despite the fact that this is a trading nation; and not only has it [England] abolished this commerce in all its dominions, but has with great fervor promoted the abolition in all nations, not even wishing to make peace without enacting such a measure" (p. 167).

The initiative was clearly that of Castlereagh, but Consalvi's own words show his [and the Holy See's] attitude towards slavery: it is described as an "inhuman commerce" (*inumano commercio*) whose abolition is demanded by the "voices of humanity and of justice" (*le voci dell'umanità e della giustizia*) (p. 167).

Consalvi noted that the argument was made that the trade was the lesser of two evils since the natives were living in a miserable state in their own countries, unable to govern themselves, etc. Castlereagh said that all such arguments were merely pretexts to cover greed, and that some people were waging wars simply to obtain title to slaves in order to sell them (p. 168).

Castlereagh requested that Consalvi ask Pope Pius VII to use his influence, especially with the Kings of Spain and Portugal, to end their slave trade. Consalvi replied that he thought the Royal Courts in question would not listen favorably to the Pope, who thought the end of that trade was indeed the will of humanity and a matter of justice, since they had not heeded his other initiatives in this regard (p. 168).

[84] Kelly, *Popes,* 307-309.

laity for whom it was written. As we will see, even today many authors do not have an accurate understanding of this work. First, however, let us consider the content of *In Supremo* itself.

The introduction of *In Supremo* tells us that it was written to turn Christians away from the practice of enslaving blacks and other peoples. Gregory first mentions the efforts of the Apostles and other early Christians to alleviate out of the motive of Christian charity the suffering of those held in servitude, and that they encouraged the practice of emancipating deserving slaves. At the same time, he notes that:

> There were to be found subsequently among the faithful some who, shamefully blinded by the desire of sordid gain, in lonely and distant countries did not hesitate to reduce to slavery (*in servitutem redigere*) Indians, Blacks and other unfortunate peoples, or else, by instituting or expanding the trade in those who had been made slaves by others, aided the crime of others. Certainly many Roman Pontiffs of glorious memory, Our Predecessors, did not fail, according to the duties of their office, to blame severely this way of acting as dangerous for the spiritual welfare of those who did such things and a shame to the Christian name.[85]

Gregory then cites the various predecessors and their antislavery teachings, even recalling the familiar phrase *in servitutem redigere* contained in the work of Paul III and his successors. He mentions the efforts of Clement I, Pius II, Paul III, Benedict XIV, Urban VIII and Pius VII, before concluding this historical summary:

> Indeed these sanctions and this concern of Our Predecessors availed in no small measure, with the help of God, to protect the Indians and the other peoples mentioned from the cruelties of the invaders and from the greed of Christian traders.[86]

---

[85] See Appendix B, No. 8.
[86] *Ibid.*, No. 8.

However, Gregory is well aware that there is still much work to be done:

> The slave trade, although it has been somewhat diminished, is still carried on by numerous Christians. Therefore, desiring to remove such a great shame from all Christian peoples... and walking in the footsteps of Our Predecessors, We, by apostolic authority, warn and strongly exhort in the Lord faithful Christians of every condition that no one in the future dare to bother unjustly, despoil of their possessions, or reduce to slavery (*in servitutem redigere*) Indians, Blacks or other such peoples. Nor are they to lend aid and favor to those who give themselves up to these practices, or exercise that inhuman traffic by which the Blacks, as if they were not humans but rather mere animals, having been brought into slavery in no matter what way, are, without any distinction and contrary to the rights of justice and humanity, bought, sold and sometimes given over to the hardest labor.[87]

Thus, the historical papal teaching against unjust servitude and the slave trade is upheld, and in 1839 is once again presented to the Christian faithful for their adherence. In Gregory's time, as with the previous papal efforts, there was obviously widespread nonacceptance on the part of Catholic clergy and laity. Thus *In Supremo* also contains a closing prohibition against clerics as well as laity who were attempting to defend slavery or the slave trade:

> We prohibit and strictly forbid any Ecclesiastic or lay person from presuming to defend as permissible this trade in Blacks under no matter what pretext or excuse, or from publishing or teaching in any manner whatsoever, in public or privately, opinions contrary to what We have set forth in these Apostolic Letters.[88]

The primary area of contention with *In Supremo* lies in determin-

---
[87] *Ibid.*, No. 8.
[88] *Ibid.*, No. 8.

ing what was actually being condemned by Gregory. The text of the Papal Constitution itself is clearly condemning *both* the slave trade *and* slavery, as is apparent from the preceding paragraph citations. Both of the above citations prohibit the *slave trade*. Likewise, in the first paragraph we read that *slavery itself* is also condemned: "... no one in the future dare to... reduce to slavery (*in servitutem redigere*) Indians, Blacks or other such peoples."[89] In the second paragraph, the prohibition of "opinions contrary to what We have set forth in these Apostolic Letters" indicates that no one may hold that slavery itself is somehow not condemned. The question that should be asked, then, is why have many bishops, historians and others interpreted *In Supremo* as condemning the slave trade, *but not slavery itself*?

Besides the quotation from Laennec Hurbon given in the first chapter,[90] we may illustrate the problem by citing also the American Church historian James Hennesey. The following is taken from his consideration of the Church's efforts, or lack thereof, to obtain the abolition of slavery in the United States:

> Opponents of slavery found slight support in official Church teaching. Pope Gregory XVI in 1838 [sic] condemned the slave trade, *but not slavery itself* [emphasis added].[91]

John T. Noonan also believes that Gregory condemned only the slave trade, and that there were exceptions even to this condemnation:

> In 1839 Gregory XVI condemned the slave trade, but not so explicitly that the condemnation covered occasional sales by owners of surplus stock.[92]

---

[89] *Ibid.*, No. 8.

[90] As noted above, Hurbon states: "But one can search in vain through the interventions of the Holy See — those of Pius V, Urban VIII, and Benedict XIV — for any condemnation of the actual principle of slavery" (Dussel, ed., *Church in Latin America*, 372).

[91] James Hennesey, S.J., *American Catholics: A History of the Roman Catholic Community in the United States* (New York: Oxford University Press, 1981), 145.

[92] Noonan, "Development," *Theological Studies* 54, 666.

The American Bishops in the last century, who were charged with applying the teaching of *In Supremo* to the slavery institution that existed in our country, as a teaching body fell into this same error regarding what was condemned:

> No [American] Catholic bishop spoke for abolition in the prewar years. In 1840 [the Bishop of Charleston] John England explained to [President Martin] Van Buren's Secretary of State, John Forsyth, that Pope Gregory XVI had condemned the trade in slaves, but that *no pope had ever condemned domestic slavery as it had existed in the United States* [emphasis added].[93]

Thus, the misreading of *In Supremo* that exists among scholars today actually has its roots in the partial rejection of that Papal Constitution by the American hierarchy over a century and a half earlier.

On the other hand, John Maxwell is quite right in his statement of what Gregory actually taught in *In Supremo*: "It is clear that the Pope is condemning unjust enslavement *and* unjust slave-trading" [emphasis added].[94] Also correct is our papal historian, J.N.D. Kelly, who states, "In the brief *In Supremo* (3 Dec. 1839) he denounced slavery *and* the slave-trade as unworthy of Christians" [emphasis added].[95]

Pius IX: *Instruction of the Holy Office, No. 1293,* June 20, 1866

Giovanni Maria Mastai-Ferretti was born May 13, 1792, and was elected Pope on June 16, 1846. Though at home Pius IX was deemed a failure politically, worldwide he achieved many successes. With his appealing personality, he has often been compared

---

[93] Hennesey, *American Catholics*, 145.
[94] Maxwell, *Slavery*, 74.
[95] Kelly, *Popes*, 308.

to Pope John XXIII. Pius signed concordats with many countries and set up over two hundred dioceses and missionary territories before his death in 1878, the longest pontificate in history. Additionally, he is remembered for his definition of the Immaculate Conception of the Blessed Virgin Mary in 1854, the "Syllabus of Errors" denouncing certain contemporary attitudes, and for calling the First Vatican Council in 1869-70, which defined papal infallibility and the compatibility of faith and reason.[96]

Instruction 1293 of the Sacred Congregation of the Holy Office, June 20, 1866,[97] was written in response to a series of questions from the Rev. William Massaia, the Vicar Apostolic of the Galla tribe in Ethiopia. The *Instruction* first describes the role slavery has in the culture of these people:

> The condition of servitude, properly so called, among the Galla and Sidama so strictly coheres with their social status that it is almost impossible to establish and maintain a home among them without the buying of slaves... Therefore the slaves are held as a principal matter of commerce; in a certain degree they have the value of money, and frequently, by the order of the leader or by prescript of their laws, creditors are held to accept them for the payment of debt.[98]

We see from this that the Holy Office was aware of how deeply ingrained slavery was in the customs and traditions of these tribes. It was not certain how the Christians living among them should act in the midst of this kind of a society, and so they sought moral guidance from the Church. Today we certainly know what the ap-

---

[96] Kelly, *Popes*, 309-310. Regarding Pius IX's views on slavery, see the Brief of July 16, 1850 issued for the beatification of Peter Claver, where the Pope called slavery a "great crime" (*summum nefas*), Brandi, *La Schiavitù*, 18. Pius IX's Brief is found in *Bullarium Societatis Jesu*, Florence, 1891, 369.

[97] The bulk of this section was taken from my article "Slavery: A Change in Church Teaching?" in *The Dunwoodie Review* 17 (1994) pp. 129-35. The other relevant sections of this lengthy *Instruction* not dealt with here may be found in Appendix C, No. 3.

[98] See Appendix C, No. 3.

propriate Christian response to any form of servitude should be, but life in Africa 130 years ago was rather different. Without condoning the practice of slavery in these communities, we can nevertheless view the response of the Holy Office which follows as a legitimate attempt to incorporate the long-standing teaching of the Church into the ancient culture of these peoples to whom the Gospel message was being delivered. This requires, however, that we be willing to look at all of the relevant sections of the Holy Office's *Instruction* in their proper verbal and social contexts.

Of the fifteen questions presented by the Vicar Apostolic to the Holy Office extensively treating this complicated issue — all of which concern the conduct of the Galla and Sidama who have been converted to the faith[99] — numbers twelve and thirteen most concern us here:

> 12. Whether it is permitted for Christians among the Galla and Sidama to buy slaves, or to receive them as payment for a debt or as a gift, as long as they act for the sake of the necessities of their home and family and without the intention of re-selling the slaves.
> 13. Whether a Christian family, not for the sake of gain, but only because of a grave means of support or the necessity of paying a debt is permitted to trade or sell a slave it possesses.[100]

After mentioning the constant efforts of the Popes to obtain the abolition of slavery, the response of the Holy Office begins:

> … servitude itself, considered in itself and all alone (*per se et absolute*), is by no means repugnant to the natural and di-

---

[99] It should be noted that *Instruction 1293* is concerned primarily with slavery among the Galla and Sidama people themselves, as indicated by Question 12: "Whether it is permitted for Christians among the Galla and Sidama to buy slaves…"
  Question 15, which does not immediately concern us here, nevertheless helps clarify the fact that the title "Christians" means the Galla and Sidama, unless used with additional reference to the European missionaries: "Whether Christians and even missionaries, can licitly be present as witnesses or agents…" (See Appendix C, No. 3).
[100] See Appendix C, No. 3.

vine law, and there can be present very many just titles for servitude, as can be seen by consulting the approved theologians and interpreters of the canons. For the dominion which belongs to a master in respect to a slave is not to be understood as any other than the perpetual right of disposing, to one's own advantage, of servile work, which dominion it is legitimate for a person to offer to another person. From this it follows that it is not repugnant to the natural and divine law that a slave be sold, bought, exchanged, or given, ...[101]

The *Instruction* is clear that the word *servitus* encompasses forms of human labor that were both acceptable in the eyes of the Church and common in some parts of the world. Given that such "just titles" for servitude exist, there also exists the right of both the one freely offering himself in servitude to be the "slave" of another and the right of the master to make use of that slave. From this the *Instruction* gives the conclusion that the buying and selling of this kind of slaves is not opposed to either divine or natural law.[102] The *Instruction* is of course referring to a very specific type of servitude, namely, one in which dominion is *offered* by one person to another, or one which follows from the various "just titles" for servitude.

The letter of the Holy Office continues, from the above block quotation:

... as long as in this sale, or buying, or exchange or giving, the due conditions which those same approved authors widely

---

[101] *Ibid.*, No. 3.

[102] In his December, 1993 article for *Theological Studies*, Judge Noonan notes of *Instruction 1293* that "The Holy Office in 1866 ruled that the buying and selling of slaves was not contrary to natural law" (*Theological Studies*, 54, ftnt. 9, 666). Noonan uses this citation as a footnote to his wide-ranging argument that the Catholic Church has changed its moral teachings on slavery and other areas to suit the changing times of society. The problem is that Noonan does not mention in that brief reference that the *Instruction* is referring to various "just titles for servitude," especially the title in which dominion is *offered* by one person to another. Forced racial slavery of the type practiced in the Western Hemisphere most certainly was not covered by any of these "just titles" for servitude, and this deserves mention whenever making reference to the *Instruction*.

> follow and explain, are properly observed. *Among these conditions those which are to be especially looked at are whether the slave who is put up for sale has been justly or unjustly deprived of his liberty*, and that the seller does nothing by which the slave to be transferred to another possessor suffer any detriment to life, morals or the Catholic faith. Therefore, Christians, about whom one is speaking in the first question [no. 12], can licitly buy slaves or, to resolve a debt, receive them as a gift, as long as they are morally certain that those slaves were not taken from their legitimate master or reduced to slavery unjustly [emphasis added].[103]

The condition that a slave must have been "justly" deprived of his liberty is essentially restating the idea that he must have *freely offered* himself in servitude, or have been enslaved as a prisoner of a just war, or as a criminal, etc. These just titles for servitude are distinct from the unjust titles for slavery, including what was, for example, practiced in the United States until the end of the Civil War. Servitude characterized by service that is offered by the slave to his master willingly, as well as by a mutual concern and respect, is known as symbiotic slavery.[104] The "just" forms of symbiotic servitude, while admittedly having much in common with our country's history of unjust racial slavery, nevertheless would more properly be compared to the former practice in America of "indentured servitude" from the 17th to the 19th centuries. This is because the indentured servant and the slave justly deprived of liberty both have chosen their lot freely. Of course, one could argue that the economic pressures of poverty forced both the indentured servant and the one justly enslaved to accept servitude against their natural preference for liberty, but such an argument does not destroy the distinction between one physically or morally forced into slavery and one freely choosing it. In the Church's mind the former was unjust, the latter could be justified.

---

[103] See Appendix C, No. 3.

[104] *The New Catholic Encyclopedia* (Washington: Catholic University of America, 1967), s.v. "Slavery (and the Church)," by. C. Williams.

It is hoped that this *Instruction* of the Holy Office is appearing to the reader to be the complex and distinction-filled document that it is. Clearly, the *Instruction* is not giving moral approbation to slavery as such, but rather is attempting to ensure that those who have become Christians among a particular group of people in one part of the world do not participate in the immoral ownership or traffic of those unjustly forced into slavery.

That this *Instruction* is giving approval to only a very specific and justifiable form of servitude may also be shown by reading the remainder of the distinctions given for dealing with those taken from their legitimate owners and those unjustly reduced to slavery. Continuing again from the block quotation above:

> For if the slaves who are offered for sale have been taken from their legitimate master, it is not permitted to buy them, because it is a crime to buy what belongs to another and has been taken, the master being unwilling, by theft. If, however, they have been unjustly reduced to slavery, then one must determine whether they are unwilling to be sold or given to Christians or whether they consent to it. If they are unwilling, they can by no means be bought or received, since the captives themselves are masters of their own liberty, although it has been unjustly taken from them. If indeed, after they have been fully taught that freedom belongs to them by right and which they lose only by injury to others, they spontaneously and by their own free will, as masters of themselves, present themselves to Christians to be received by them and held in their servitude... in such circumstances it is permissible for the Christians, especially when they act in favor of the faith, to purchase such captives for a just price, and to take and retain them in their own servitude, as long as they are of the mind to treat them according to the precepts of Christian charity, and take care to imbue them with the rudiments of the faith...[105]

---

[105] See Appendix C, No. 3.

The *Instruction* here condemns first: stealing, for the purpose of sale, slaves taken from their "legitimate master," meaning, of course, one who possesses slaves who have been justly and/or freely taken into servitude. For those unjustly enslaved, the Holy Office first teaches that what little freedom they still have must be preserved by allowing them to decide for themselves if they wish to improve their condition by entering instead into the service of Christians. Only those who freely give their consent may be purchased by a Christian, and then they must be treated with Christian love and offered the opportunity to receive the Faith. These distinctions have their foundation, indeed were quoted almost verbatim, from an *Instruction* (*No. 515*) of Pope Pius VI given through the Holy Office over one hundred years earlier to Christians encountering similar difficulties in Cambodia.[106]

The next sections concerns the second of the two questions asked in the beginning, that of whether Christians may sell slaves they possess:

> Indeed, just as slaves can be licitly bought, so they can licitly also be sold, but it is altogether necessary that the seller is the legitimate possessor of the slave, and does nothing in the sale by which the life, morals or Catholic faith of the slave to be sold would be harmed. Therefore it is illicit to sell a slave or in any manner give the slave into the ownership of any master who by a certain or probable judgment can be foreseen to treat that slave inhumanely, or lead him to sin or abuse him for the sake of that most evil trade which has been condemned and strictly prohibited by the constitutions of the Roman pontiffs, especially by Pope Gregory XVI. Likewise it is illicit to sell a slave, taking no account of the marriage rights and duties of that same slave. Much more illicit is it to sell a Christian slave to a faithless master, or even, where the danger of falling away is prudently to be feared, to a heretical or schismatic master.[107]

---

[106] See Appendix C, No. 2.
[107] *Ibid.*, No. 3.

In the sale of a slave, we see again that he must first have been possessed legitimately, that is, held by one engaged solely in symbiotic or other forms of servitude under a "just title," and that the sale to a different owner not result in his physical, moral or spiritual detriment. Examples of such types of harm include sale to masters or traders engaged in unjust slavery, or sale to those who would not respect the marital and spiritual rights of the slave. That the *Instruction* refers to the teaching of Gregory XVI's *In Supremo* shows that it wishes to confirm the consistent papal teaching against unjust slavery and the slave trade in force since the 15th century.[108]

The final section to be cited, so that consideration may be given to the entirety of the *Instruction* relevant to our present discussion, answers the question of whether slaves have the right to escape if they are able:

> Regularly it is the right of slaves who have been unjustly reduced to slavery to flee; it is not permitted for slaves who undergo just servitude, unless perhaps they are solicited by the master to some sin, or are treated inhumanly.[109]

We see that the Holy Office defended the right of those unjustly held as slaves to flee. Thus, those slaves held in the United States would have been justified in their attempts to escape, since they were being held unjustly. This teaching of the Church is of course in opposition to the position taken by most of the American bishops, who taught that slaves may not attempt to escape from their masters. Additionally, those held according to one of the just titles to servitude may likewise seek their freedom by escape if they are being abused, as was often the case, or are being encouraged to engage in some sinful activity.

I do not like much of the content of this Holy Office *Instruction*. I find it in a certain sense haunting and indeed, revolting, by today's standards of personal equality, liberty and justice. Never-

---

[108] See Appendix B, No. 8.
[109] See Appendix C, No. 3.

theless the real meaning of the document must not remain unchallenged in the hands of those who wish to construe its meaning to fit questionable conclusions. Without explaining the *Instruction* away we may rather look upon it as a legitimate attempt to address a complicated issue. Nothing immoral was given approbation by the Holy Office. Rather a positive morality was presented that both allowed the Christian converts to continue to live among the Galla and Sidama tribes in spite of their "culture of slavery," and encouraged those same Christians to improve in a real way the plight of the enslaved. This was because these slaves were allowed to be taken into the service of Christian owners, as long as the numerous conditions of physical, moral and spiritual well-being were respected, and most importantly, that the type of servitude practiced was just. In fact the document is in keeping with the previous condemnations, issued by several popes from the 15th to the 19th centuries, of unjust forms of servitude.[110]

Leo XIII: *In Plurimis* and *Catholicae Ecclesiae*

These works of Pope Leo XIII were written at the close of the era of slavery and are readily available in both Latin and English.[111] Thus the actual texts of these encylicals are not included in the appendix, but a general treatment of their content is certainly deserved. *Catholicae Ecclesiae* contains the sole new development by way of the Papal Magisterium's teaching against slavery. However, both of these encyclicals are primarily concerned with remov-

---

[110] Clearly then, it is not acceptable for Noonan to cite a small section of a teaching as detailed and controversial as *Instruction 1293* without explaining also the qualifications of time and place and the context of previous teachings, as well as those essential distinctions made within the document itself.

[111] *In Plurimis* — See the following: *Acta Leonis XIII*, III:69-84; *Acta Sanctae Sedis*, 20:545-59; Claudia Carlen, *The Papal Encyclicals: 1878-1903* (Raleigh: McGrath, 1981), 159-167.
  Catholicae Ecclesiae — See the following: *Acta Leonis XIII*, IV:112-16; *Acta Sanctae Sedis*, 23:257-260; Carlen, *Papal Encyclicals: 1878-1903*, 233-235.

ing the last vestiges of slavery from the face of the earth, and thus provide an appropriate ending to the pontiffs' consistent efforts across the centuries to bring an end to this great injustice.

In Plurimis, May 5, 1888

Pope Leo issued *In Plurimis* to encourage the Bishops of Brazil to do all they could to ensure that the abolition of slavery, which had just been legally attained, was actually put into effect. Most of *In Plurimis* consists of an historical summary of slavery in the world. The original sin of Adam first made it possible for the world to fall into the condition of servitude. With the supernatural redemption wrought in Christ, the new Adam, mankind was given the divine guidance and grace to at first alleviate the sufferings of slaves, and soon, to work towards securing their earthly freedom as well. Leo then mentions the efforts of the early Christians and Church Fathers to offer kind and just treatment, as well as religious instruction, to those held in servitude. This teaching was not intended to change the institution immediately, but rather gave the world the impetus and constant support for gradually achieving that end: "The care of the Church extended to the protection of slaves, and without interruption tended carefully to one object, that they should finally be restored to freedom, which would be greatly conducive to their eternal welfare."[112]

The efforts of Leo's predecessors to prevent slavery in the newly discovered territories of Africa, Asia and America are then reviewed, with Leo noting that there has been obtained "thanks to Our constant pleadings, some satisfaction for the long-continued and most just complaints of nature and religion."[113] A plea is then made to end the problem of the continuing slave trade in Africa, where approximately 400,000 Africans were captured and sold like livestock each year:

---

[112] Leo XIII, *Catholicae Ecclesiae*, No. 12, Carlen, *Encyclicals, 1878-1903*, 163.
[113] *Ibid.*, p. 165.

> Would that all who hold high positions in authority and power, or who desire the rights of nations and of humanity to be held sacred, or who earnestly devote themselves to the interests of Catholic religion, would all, everywhere acting on Our exhortations and wishes, strive together to repress, forbid, and put an end to that kind of traffic, than which nothing is more base and wicked.[114]

With the support of the Emperor Dom Pedro II, Brazil had achieved the abolition of the slave trade in 1850, the children of slaves were declared born free in 1871, and in 1888 all legal slavery had been brought to an end. Pope Leo then asked the Bishops of Brazil to continue to press for an end to the actual practice of slavery, but asks that this occur peacefully:

> It is, however, chiefly to be wished that this may be prosperously accomplished, which all desire, that slavery may be banished and blotted out without any injury to divine or human rights, with no political agitation, and so with the solid benefit of the slaves themselves, for whose sake it is undertaken.[115]

Catholicae Ecclesiae, **November 20, 1890**

Catholicae Ecclesiae is written to the bishops of the world, asking them to work to bring about an end to slavery in Africa and the evangelization of that continent, especially through the financial support of the missions. This latter work states that all men are "created one in origin, redeemed by the same price and called to the same eternal happiness."[116] This is a movement beyond previous pontifical statements in that equality is taught to be grounded

---

[114] *Ibid.*, p. 166.

[115] *Ibid.*, p.166.

[116] "... *utpote eadem origine cretos [sic], eodem pretio redemptos, ad eamdem vocatos beatitatem aeternam...*": *Acta Leonis XIII*, IV:112.

not only in redemption and vocation, but also in origin. Furthermore, there is contained herein a succinct statement of the Popes' efforts to improve the plight of slaves and to oppose the institution of slavery itself.[117] This task began with the teaching and example of Christ Himself, and was entrusted to the Apostles and their successors, especially the successors of Peter:

> Insofar as time and circumstances allowed, [Christ] gradually and moderately accomplished His goal... The zeal of the Church for liberating the slaves has not languished with the

---

[117] With Leo XIII, Maxwell believes there was a change in the Magisterium's attitude toward the institution of slavery:
"The significance of these two letters of Pope Leo XIII is that it was no longer individual Catholics, whether lay or clerical who were expressing 'anti-slavery' sentiments, it was the Pope himself... No distinction was made between just and unjust enslavement; it was the institution as such which was equivalently condemned. Pope Leo XIII offered no explanation for this change of theological attitude" (*Slavery*, 118-119).
    Maxwell once again does not accept the historically licit "just titles" to servitude (see Chapter One). In this case, it leads him to believe Leo XIII's teaching to be a departure from that of his predecessors because he says the Pope does not distinguish between just and unjust servitude. However, the only teachings of the popes against slavery which makes such distinctions are found in *Instructions 515* and *1293* of the Holy Office. All of the other popes we have been considering, including Leo XIII, were clearly "expressing antislavery sentiments" because they were opposing unjust servitude (which is of course the equivalent term for the slavery which was practiced in the Western Hemisphere for four centuries). Thus in both of his works, Leo cited the efforts of his predecessors against such slavery because he agreed with their teachings, and not because he wished to depart from them.
    Consistent to the end, Maxwell closes his consideration of Church teaching on slavery with the following comment regarding the "corrections" made by the Second Vatican Council:
"It will be noticed that there was no attempt to draw any distinctions concerning the titles of slave-ownership in Roman civil law. From this it may be *assumed* that slavery even as a penalty for crime is considered as morally unlawful" [emphasis added] (*Slavery*, 125).
This argument from silence is weak indeed. Throughout his work, Maxwell is preoccupied with attempting to show that the Roman pontiffs failed to condemn the just titles to servitude until 1888 or later. In the process, Maxwell himself fails to realize the tremendous positive value contained in the consistent antislavery teachings of the popes. Actually, aside from the particular situations treated in the *Instructions* of the Holy Office, the just titles were of little consequence for the papal teaching against slavery in the Americas. What was relevant was rather *the unjust slavery itself* that the Indians and Blacks were being subjected to in South and North America, and it is just such slavery that the many popes clearly and consistently condemned.

passage of time; on the contrary the more it bore fruit, the more eagerly it glowed. There are incontestable historical documents which attest to that fact, documents which commended to posterity the names of many of Our predecessors. Among them St. Gregory the Great, Hadrian I, Alexander III, Innocent III, Gregory IX, Pius II, Leo X, Paul III, Urban VIII, Benedict XIV, Pius VII, and Gregory XVI stand out. They applied every effort to eliminate the institution of slavery wherever it existed. They also took care lest the seeds of slavery return to those places from which this evil institution had been cut away.[118]

Special recognition is given to Cardinal Charles Lavigerie (1825-1892), the founder of the Society of Missionaries in Africa. The White Fathers, as they became known, began the work of converting Africa in 1869. Lavigerie worked tirelessly for the upbuilding of his new order, enduring and overcoming many difficulties caused by climate, the French government and his own poor health. Many missions were undertaken, including the building of refuges for slave children. Lavigerie was created a cardinal by Pope Leo XIII in 1881, who in writing *In Plurimis* (1888) borrowed passages verbatim from Lavigerie's own pastoral letter encouraging the suppression of slavery. In *Catholicae Ecclesiae* (1890), Leo gave the Cardinal the task of bringing Europe to agree to end "this gloomy plague of slavery" in Africa:

> We have immediately delegated the task of going to the principal countries of Europe to Our beloved son Charles Martial Cardinal Lavigerie, whose swiftness and apostolic zeal are well known. He is to show how shameful this base dealing is and to incline the leaders to assist this miserable race.[119]

Leo then thanks the leaders of Europe for the progress already made to eradicate slavery, especially through their meeting together in

---

[118] Leo XIII, *Catholicae Ecclesiae*, No. 1, Carlen, *Encyclicals, 1878-1903*, 233.
[119] *Ibid.*, p. 234.

Brussels earlier that year. Donald Attwater notes in his book on the White Fathers that Cardinal Lavigerie had a large part in that meeting:

> Throughout 1888 and 1889 [Lavigerie] travelled from country to country, appealing to the nations of Europe to put an end to the traffic in human beings and its hideous cruelties: he addressed a large meeting in London, under the chairmanship of Lord Granville and with Cardinal Manning and several Anglican bishops on the platform, and at the international conference in Brussels in 1890 his practical suggestions towards abolishing the trade were adopted almost as a whole. "If inner Africa is to be saved the anger of the world must first be aroused," he said, and nothing did more towards that end than the burning words of Cardinal Lavigerie.[120]

Pope Leo is aware of the close connection between liberty and the Gospel. He notes that the most important task is for the missionaries to spread that Good News "because those who have received this light have also shaken off the yoke of human slavery."[121] To that end, a collection is established to be taken up each year around the world on the feast of the Epiphany of the Lord. The Congregation for the Propagation of the Faith is to distribute those funds to the missions in Africa specifically for the purpose of eradicating slavery through the truth of the Gospel message.

---

[120] Donald Attwater, *The White Fathers in Africa* (London: Burns Oates and Washbourne Ltd., 1937), pp. 13-14.
[121] Leo XIII, *Catholicae Ecclesiae*, No. 3, cited from Carlen, *Encyclicals, 1878-1903*, 234.

CHAPTER THREE

Conclusion

We began this study by noting the relatively late date that many authors assign to the Church's formal condemnation of slavery, including John T. Noonan, who stated that "Only in 1890 did Pope Leo XIII attack the institution [of slavery] itself."[122] Likewise, of the 1888 and 1890 works of Leo, Maxwell comments:

> "Clearly, this was already about 100 years too late to be of any effective value in the antislavery campaigns and civil wars and revolutions of the nineteenth century; the lay reformers and abolitionists had won their campaigns without much effective help or moral leadership from the teaching authority of the Catholic Church which had hitherto consistently refused to condemn the institution of slavery or the practice of slave-trading as such."[123]

It is true that the teaching of the Church likely had little influence in the United States in bringing an end to slavery, for reasons which we will consider. However, it is simply inaccurate to say that the teaching authority of the Catholic Church did not provide the needed teaching against slavery and the slave trade until such a late date as these and other authors assert.

---

[122] See ftnt. 1.
[123] Maxwell, *Slavery*, 119.

From the documents we have considered, it is clear that the forced enslavement of Indians and Blacks was condemned from the time that the "Age of Discovery" began, and that as this problem continued and expanded in the territorial finds of the New World, the same teaching of the Roman pontiffs was reiterated time and again. Likewise, the buying and selling of slaves unjustly held was also condemned by 1435. The development of this teaching over the span of nearly five centuries was occasioned by the unique and illicit form of servitude that accompanied the Age of Discovery. The just titles to servitude were not rejected by the Church, but rather were tolerated for many reasons. This in no way invalidates the clear and consistent teaching against the unjust slavery that came to prevail in Africa and the Western Hemisphere, first in Central and South America and then in the United States, for approximately four centuries.

Special mention must be made once again of the ground breaking efforts of Pope Paul III in the early sixteenth century. In *Sublimis Deus*, he taught all Christians of his and every future age that all people are equal due to their calling to receive the faith and eternal life. From this, Paul taught the world that:

> ... the same Indians and all other peoples, even though they are outside the faith, who shall hereafter come to the knowledge of Christians are not to have been deprived or be deprived of their liberty of their possessions. Rather, they are to be able to use and enjoy this liberty and this ownership of property freely and licitly, and are not to be reduced to slavery (*nec in servitutem redigi debere*).[124]

As shown in the course of this paper, *Sublimis* then served as the basis of the consistent Church teachings for the New World. These teachings both condemned the action of reducing the newly found peoples to slavery, and commanded that the Christian faith be presented to them without exception. Over the course of the next three

---
[124] Appendix B, No. 2.

and a half centuries, the Church's teaching remained consistently opposed to the enslavement of these peoples, and was applied to various parts of the world as was deemed necessary. *Sublimis* is even held by many to be the foundational work for the subsequent development of international law. The only "change" that occurred in its teaching was the expansion by Pope Leo XIII of the reasons for the evil of slavery. To the previous teaching on the redemption of all people and the universal call to the faith and eternal salvation, Leo added the reason of the unity of human origins.

In the *Harvard Theological Review*, Lewis Hanke gave the following praise to this "momentous bull," *Sublimis Deus*:

> In issuing this bull Paul III was following the established tradition of the Christian Church. From its earliest day Christianity had proclaimed in the most solemn and excellent terms the absolute spiritual equality and brotherhood of all men.[125]

In *Pastorale Officium* the same antislavery teaching was presented, and was coupled with the penalty of excommunication for violations of its precepts. Remarkably, though *Pastorale* was revoked, it continued to influence the development of the Magisterium's teaching and the practice of attaching penalties to that teaching. Of *Pastorale Officium*, Maxwell states: "It is a pity that Denzinger quotes a document which was annulled a year after its publication."[126] However, not only *Denzinger-Schönmetzer*, but also Urban VIII, Benedict XIV, Gregory XVI and Leo XIII were to make reference to this Bull. They either did not know of the subsequent revocation of *Pastorale*, or simply chose to ignore that revocation in favor of the valid teaching it contained. Indeed, we can agree with Gutierrez's statement on both the importance of these works of Paul III, as well as the irrelevance, practically speaking, of the 1538 revocation of *Pastorale Officium*:

---

[125] Hanke, "Pope Paul III," *Review*, XXX, 73.

> ... we must forthrightly accept the fact that the documents of Paul III — in a special way *Sublimis Deus*; *Altitudo Divini Consilii*, of course; and even *Pastorale Officium* — are part of the Magisterium of the Church. Paul III's revocatory brief *Non Indecens* did not leave a mark on the Church's official teaching.[127]

Mention must also be made of the teaching of the later popes that not only the faith of the Catholic Church, but also her protecting arm, should be extended to all people. Benedict XIV saw the foundation for this teaching in the example of Christ himself:

> The immense charity of the Prince of Pastors, Jesus Christ, who came so that men might have life more abundantly and gave Himself as redemption for the many, urges us, as we unworthily serve as His vicar on earth, to have no greater charity than to strive to lay down our life not only for Christ's faithful but also for all men whatsoever...[128]

The substantial teaching against slavery that was provided by the Papal Magisterium rightly should give Catholics, and indeed all Christians, a great sense of pride. This teaching was founded in the teachings of Our Lord that all people are loved immensely by God the Father, and have received redemption and the vocation to eternal happiness in Christ the Son. At the same time, it must be remembered that Christians themselves, and notably members of the clergy, frequently and sometimes blatantly violated this same teaching. Nevertheless, the Catholic tradition of opposition to unjust servitude was a great help in eventually bringing about an end to the enslavement of the Indians and Blacks in many parts of Latin America, as well as of the peoples in the Philippines and other areas.

---

[126] *Slavery*, 69.
[127] Gutierrez, *Las Casas*, 312.
[128] See Appendix B, No. 7.

In the United States the results were certainly far less impressive. The American institution of slavery that began in the early 17th century and continued to expand through the first half of the 19th, was to be dismantled only through the bloodshed of the Civil War. Why were the teachings of the Church not more effective in the cause of eradicating slavery in this country? One could argue that it was because the United States was not a "Catholic country," unlike the nations of Latin America. Indeed, in the decade before *In Supremo* there were only three hundred and eighteen thousand Catholics in the United States.[129] Also, the abolition movement was dominated by anti-Catholic nativists, which certainly deterred Catholics from joining their ranks.[130]

The prevalent attitude of the American hierarchy, with some notable exceptions in both directions, was that many aspects of slavery were evil, but that to change the law would be, practically speaking, a greater evil. Some put forth strong arguments in favor of the institution of slavery, such as Bishop John England of Charleston, who believed it to be among the accepted practices of the early Church:

> The right of the master, the duty of the slave, the lawfulness of continuing the relations, and the benevolence of religion in mitigating the sufferings ... are the results exhibited by our view of the laws and facts during the first four centuries of Christianity.[131]

Answering the charge that Catholics were widely supporting the abolitionist movement — which sadly was far from accurate — England noted that Gregory XVI was condemning only the *slave trade* and *not slavery itself*, especially as it existed in the United States. To prove his opinion, England had *In Supremo* translated

---

[129] Hennesey, *American Catholics*, 5.

[130] Michael V. Gannon, *Rebel Bishop: The Life and Era of Augustin Verot* (Milwaukee: Bruce Publishing Company, 1964), 39.

[131] *Ibid.*, 35.

and published in his diocesan newspaper, *The United States Catholic Miscellany*, and even went so far as to write a series of eighteen extensive letters to John Forsyth, the Secretary of State under President Martin Van Buren, to explain how he and most of the other American bishops interpreted *In Supremo*. In one of these letters we learn of the events of the 1840 Council of Baltimore, where the bishops read and discussed this Apostolic Letter:

> Thus, if this document condemned our domestic slavery as an unlawful and consequently immoral practice, the bishops could not have accepted it without being bound to refuse the sacraments to all who were slave holders unless they manumitted their slaves; yet, if you look to the prelates who accepted the document, for the acceptation was immediate and unanimous: you will find, 1st the Archbishop of Baltimore... 2d, the Bishop of Bardstown... 3d, the Bishop of Charleston... 4th, the Bishop of St. Louis... 5th, the Bishop of Mobile... 6th, the Bishop of New Orleans... and, 7th the Bishop of Nashville... they all regarded the letter as treating of the 'slave-trade,' and not as touching 'domestic slavery.' I believe, sir, we may consider this to be pretty conclusive evidence as to the light in which that document is viewed by the Roman Catholic Church.[132]

Amazingly, it was decided that papal pronouncements against slavery, particularly Gregory XVI's *In Supremo*, did not apply to the institution as it existed in the United States, thus yielding on this issue a sort of Americanized Gallicanism. However, it is clear that Gregory wrote *In Supremo* to condemn precisely what was occurring in the United States, namely the enslavement of Blacks:

> We, by apostolic authority, warn and strongly exhort in the Lord faithful Christians of every condition that no one in the future dare to bother unjustly, despoil of their possessions, or

---

[132] Ignatius Aloysius Reynolds, editor, *The Works of the Right Rev. John England, III* (Baltimore: John Murphy & Co., 1849), Letter II, 116-117.

reduce to slavery (*in servitutem redigere*) Indians, Blacks or other such peoples.[133]

England evidently felt that justification for this dissent lay in the episcopal [mis]interpretation of *In Supremo*.

Likewise, Francis Patrick Kenrick, who was made the Archbishop of Baltimore, agreed with England on the legitimacy of slavery based on Scripture and the facts of history,[134] and believed changing the law would bring more harm than good for those held in slavery:

> Nevertheless, since this is the state of things, nothing should be tried against the laws, or be done or said that would make them carry their yoke unwillingly: but rather prudence and charity of the holy ministers [clergy] should be shown in such a way that slaves, informed by Christian custom, should offer obedience to their masters.[135]

These arguments are not dissimilar to the widespread dissent from the Church's teachings against slavery by bishops, priests and laity that was common from the 17th to 19th centuries. For the Catholics of the United States — as for Catholics everywhere — there was the consistent historical teaching of the Church, as presented through Eugene IV, Pius II, Paul III, Gregory XIV, Urban VIII, Innocent XI, Benedict XIV, Pius VII and others. For the early 19th century, in the midst of the volatile decades before the Civil War, Gregory XVI issued *In Supremo*, with its clear condemnation of both the slave trade and slavery itself. Since that Constitution mentioned the documents of the previous pontiffs, it is hard to

---

[133] See Appendix B, No. 8.

[134] *Ibid.*, 35.

[135] Francis Patrick Kenrick, *Theologia Moralis*, I (Philadelphia, 1841), 257: "*Caeterum quum ea sit rerum conditio, nihil contra leges tendandum est, nec quid quo servi in libertatem vindicentur, vel quo jugum aegre ferant, faciendum vel dicendum; sed prudentia et charitas sacrorum ministrorum in eo exhibendae, ut servi, moribus christianis informati, dominis praestent obsequia.*"

understand how the American hierarchy was not aware of the consistency of the teaching and its nature. All of these teachings nonetheless went unknown to the Catholic faithful of the U.S., perhaps through willed ignorance, or were explained away by many of the American bishops and clergy. Thus we can look to the practice of non-compliance with the teachings of the Papal Magisterium as a key reason why slavery was not directly opposed by the Church in the United States.

Undoubtedly, much can be learned from the consideration of an issue such as the Church's teaching on slavery, which involves the fields of dogma, morality and Church history. Perhaps we can take away from this consideration for our day a certain earned respect and appreciation for the wonderful gift Christ has left us in the teaching office of His Church. We see here the consistency of the Church's moral teaching against slavery, and the positive doctrinal development of the principle of the equality of all peoples. Through the Papal Magisterium, many popes taught time and again that respect must be shown for the right of each individual to be free and to come to a knowledge of the Faith. Through the episcopal magisterium of such bishops as Las Casas and Lavigerie this teaching was developed and applied to each area of the world, not without at least some positive results. Without the Papal Magisterium's efforts to guide and direct the actions of the many Christians who made history in the world, especially in this "New World," the facts of that history would indeed have been substantially altered for the worse.

Though the oppressive *institution* of slavery has at last been virtually abolished from the world, it is obvious that such servitude has managed to take a new and more subtle form. Today, even in our own country we see forms of servitude, especially in the case of undocumented illegal aliens in many fields and sweatshops. We have also witnessed prominent political figures who do not pay just social security for their foreign employees. Unfortunately, even some who strive for the causes of social justice, equality and a general liberation of the world from the errors of the past, at the same time perpetuate on a silent minority injustice, inequality, and a re-

fusal to repent of the obvious failures of history. In this, they seek to reduce humanity to a slavery of promiscuity and selfishness, and thereby advocate a most serious disrespect for the well-being of one another, most especially of the unborn, the young and of women. After nearly twenty-five years of legalized abortion and half a century of readily available contraceptives, might we ask ourselves what role the Church should exercise in freeing Christians from these failed attempts at "liberation"? Twenty-five years after Paul VI issued *Humane Vitae*, are there similarities in the situation of our day to that of the last century, when consistent papal teaching against slavery was ignored or explained away by those mandated to lead the Catholic faithful? Until questions such as these are addressed, the full teaching of Christ's Church may remain unknown to many of those who seek the Truth that will indeed set them free.

Appendix A

Chronology

Spanish Conquest of Canary Islands	1404
Sicut Dudum, Eugene IV	1435
European Discovery of New World	1492
Letters of Alexander VI	1493
Cortes Defeats the Aztecs	1521
The Only Way, Bartolome de Las Casas	1534
Paul III	1537
Sublimis Deus	
Pastorale Officium	
Altitudo Divini	
European Conquest of Philippines	1521
Council of Trent	1545-63
Cum Sicuti, Gregory XIV	1591
North American Settlement at Jamestown	1607
Commissum Nobis, Urban VIII	1639
Holy Office *Instruction 230* (Africa)	1686
Immensa Pastorum, Benedict XIV	1741
American Independence	1776
Holy Office *Instruction 515* (Indochina)	1776
Pius VII, Congress of Vienna	1814-15
Slavery Outlawed in British Colonies	1833
In Supremo, Gregory XVI	1839
United States Emancipation of Slaves Declared	1863
Holy Office *Instruction 1293* (Galla tribe in Africa)	1866
In Plurimis, Leo XIII	1888
Slavery Outlawed in Brazil	1888
Catholicae Ecclesiae, Leo XIII	1890

APPENDIX B

Documents of the Papal Magisterium Against Slavery

NUMBER ONE:

Eugene IV: *Sicut Dudum*, January 13, 1435. Found in Baronius' *Annales Ecclesiastici*, ed. O. Raynaldus (Luca, 1752) vol. 28, pp. 226-227.

Venerabilibus fratribus Pacem etc.

Sicut dudum venerabilis fratris nostri Fernandi Robicensis episcopi inter Christifideles, ac habitatores insularum Canariae interpretis, et ab eis ad sedem Apostolicam nuncii destinati, aliorumque fideidignorum insinuatione intelleximus; licet in insulis praedictis quaedam de Lancellot nuncupata, et nonnullae aliae circumadiacentes insulae, quarum habitatores et incolae solam legem naturalem imitantes, nullan antea infidelium nec haereticorum sectam noverant a paucis citra temporibus, divina cooperante clementia, ad orthodoxam catholicam fidem sint reductae, pro eo tamen, quod labente tempore, in quibusdam aliis ex praedictis insulis gubernatores ac defensores idonei, qui illarum habitatores et incolas in spiritualibus et temporalibus ad

To our venerable brothers, peace and Apostolic benediction, etc.

Not long ago we learned from our brother Ferdinand, bishop at Rubicon and representative of the faithful who are residents of the Canary Islands and from messengers sent by them to the Apostolic See, and from other trustworthy informers the following facts: in said islands — some called Lanzarote — and other nearby islands, the inhabitants, imitating the natural law alone and not having known previously any sect of apostates or heretics, have a short time since been led into the orthodox Catholic faith with the aid of God's mercy. Nevertheless, with the passage of time it has happened that in some of the said islands, because of a lack of suitable governors and defenders to direct those who live there to a proper observance of the faith in

rectam fidei observantiam dirigerent, ac eorum res et bona concite tuerentur defuerunt, nonnulli Christiani, quod dolenter referimus, diversis confictis coloribus et captatis occasionibus, ad praefatas insulas cum eorum navigiis, manu armata accedentes, plures inibi etiam juxta ipsorum simplicitatem, incaute repertos utriusque sexus homines, nonnullos iam tunc baptismatis unda renatos, et alios ex eis sub spe, ac pollicitatione, quod eos vellent sacramento baptismatis insignire, etiam quandoque fraudulenter et deceptorie, securitatis fide promissa, et non servata, secum captivos, etiam ad partes cismarinas duxerunt, bonis eorum praedae expositis, seu in eorum usus, et utilitatem conversis, nonnullos quoque ex habitatoribus et incolis praedictis subdiderunt perpetuae servituti, ac aliquos personis aliis vendiderunt, et alias contra eos diversa illicita et nefaria commiserunt, propter quae quamplurimi ex residuis dictarum insualarum habitatoribus servitutem huiusmodi plurimum execrantes, prioribus erroribus remanent involuti, se propterea ab suscipiendi baptismatis proposito retrahentes, in gravem Divinae majestatis offensam, et animarum periculum, ac Christianae religionis non modicum detrimentum.

things spiritual and temporal and to protect valiantly their property and goods, some Christians (we speak of this with sorrow), with fictitious reasoning and seizing an opportunity, have approached said islands by ship and with armed forces, taken captive and even carried off to lands overseas very many persons of both sexes, taking advantage of their simplicity. Some of these people were already baptized; others were even at times tricked and deceived by the hope and promise of Baptism, having been made a promise of safety which was not kept. They have deprived the natives of their property or turned it to their own use, and have subjected some of the inhabitants of said islands to perpetual slavery, (*subdiderunt perpetuae servituti*) sold them to other persons and committed other various illicit and evil deeds against them, because of which very many of those remaining on said islands and condemning such slavery have remained involved in their former errors, having drawn back from their intention to receive Baptism, thus offending the majesty of God, putting their souls in danger, and causing no little harm to the Christian religion.

Therefore We, to whom it pertains, especially in respect to the aforesaid matters, to rebuke

Appendix B

Nos igitur, ad quos pertinet, praesertim in praemissis, et circa ea, peccatorem quemlibes corrigere de peccato, non volentes ex sub dissimulatione transire, ac cupientes, prout ex debito pastoralis tenemur officii, quantum possumus, salubriter providere, ac ipsorum habitatorum et incolarum afflictionibus pio et paterno compatientes affectu, universos et singulos, principes temporales, dominos, capitaneos, armigeros, barones, milites, nobiles, communitates, et alios quoscumque Christifideles cuiuscumque status, gradus, vel conditionis fuerint, obsecramus in Domino, et per aspersionem Sanguinis Jesu Christi exhortamur, eisque in remissionem suorum peccaminum injungimus, ut et ipsi a praemissis desistant, et eorum subditos a talibus retrahant, rigideque compescant. Et nihilominus universis, et singulis eisdem utriusque sexus Christifidelibus praecipimur, et mandamus, quatenus infra quindecim dierum spatium a die publictionis praesentium in loco, in quo ipsi degunt faciendae computandorum, omnes et singulos utriusque sexus dictarum insularum olim habitatores Canarios nuncupatos, tempore captionis eorum captos, quos servituti subditos habent, pristinae restituant libertati, ac totaliter

each sinner about his sin, and not wishing to pass by dissimulating, and desiring — as is expected from the pastoral office we hold — as far as is possible, to provide salutarily, with a holy and fatherly concern, for the sufferings of the inhabitants, beseech in the Lord and exhort, through the sprinkling of the Blood of Jesus Christ shed for their sins, one and all, temporal princes, lords, captains, armed men, barons, soldiers, nobles, communities and all others of every kind among the Christian faithful of whatever state, grade or condition that they themselves desist from the aforementioned deeds, cause those subject to them to desist from them, and restrain them rigorously. And no less do We order and command all and each of the faithful of each sex that, within the space of fifteen days of the publication of these letters in the place where they live, that they restore to their earlier liberty all and each person of either sex who were once residents of said Canary Islands and made captives since the time of their capture and who have been made subject to slavery. These people are to be totally and perpetually free and are to be let go without the exaction or reception of any money. If this is not done, when the fifteen days have passed, they incur the sentence of excommuni-

liberos perpetuo esse et absque aliquarum pecuniarum exactione sive receptione, abire dimittant, alioquin lapsis diebus eisdem excommunicationis sententiam ipso facto incurrent, a qua nec apud sedem Apostolicam, vel per archiepiscopum Hispatensem protempore existentem, seu Fernandum episcopum antedictum, ac nisi personis captivatis huiusmodi prius et ante omnia libertati deditis, et bonis eorum primitus restitutis, absolvi nequeant, praeterquam in mortis articulo constituti. Similem excommunicationis sententiam incurrere volumus omnes et singulos, qui eosdem Canarios baptizatos, aut ad baptismum voluntarie venientes, capere, aut vendere, vel servituti subiicere attentabunt, a qua aliter, quam ut praefertur, nequeant absolutionis beneficium obtinere. Illi vero, qui exhortationibus, et mandatis nostris huiusmodi humiliter paruerint cum effectu, praeter nostram et Apostolicae sedis gratiam, et benedictionem, quam proinde uberius consequantur, aeternae beatitudinis professores fieri mereantur, et a dextris Dei cum electis, perpetua requie collocari, etc. Dat. Florentiae anno incarnationis Dominicae MCDXXXV, id. januarii.

cation *ipso facto*, from which they cannot be absolved, except at the point of death, even by the Holy See or by any [Spanish] bishop or by the aforementioned Ferdinand unless they have first given freedom to these captive persons and restored their goods. We will that like sentence of excommunication be incurred by one and all who attempt to capture or sell or subject to slavery (*servituti subicere*) baptized residents of the Canary Islands or those who are freely seeking Baptism, from which excommunication they cannot be absolved except as was stated above. Those who humbly and efficaciously obey these our exhortations and commands deserve, in addition to our favor and that of the Apostolic See, and the blessings which follow therefrom, are to be possessors of eternal happiness and to be placed in perpetual rest at the right hand of God, etc. Given at Florence, January 13, 1435 A.D.

NUMBER TWO:

Paul III: *Sublimis Deus,* June 2, 1537. Found in *Las Casas En Mexico: Historia y obras desconocidas,* by Helen-Rand Parish and Harold E. Weidman, Mexico City: Fondo De Cultura Economica, 1992, pp. 310-311.

Paulus Episcopus, servus servorum Dei, Universis Christi fidelibus praesentes litteras inspecturis, Salutem et Apostolicam benedictionem.

   Sublimis Deus sic delexit humanum genus, ut hominem talem condiderit qui non solum boni sicut ceterae creaturae particeps esset, sed ipsum Summum inaccesibile et invisibile Bonum attingere et facie ad faciem videre posset. Et cum homo ad vitam et beatitudinem eternam obeundam etiam Sacrarum Scripturarum testimonio creatus sit et hanc vitam et beatitudinem aeternam nemo consequi valeat nisi perfidem Domini nostri Jesu Christi — fateri necesse est hominem talis conditionis et naturae esse ut Fidem Christi recipere possit, et quemcumque, qui naturam hominis sortitus est, ad ipsam Fidem recipiendam habilem esse. Nec enim quisquam adeo desipere creditur, ut sese credat finem obtinere posse et medium summe necessarium nequaquam attingere.

   Hinc Veritas ipsa quae nec falli, nec fallere potest, cum Praedictores

The Bishop Paul, servant of the servants of God, to all the faithful who will read these letters, health and the Apostolic benediction.

   The exalted God loved the human race so much that He created man in such a condition that he was not only a sharer in good as are other creatures, but also that he would be able to reach and see face to face the inaccessible and invisible Supreme Good. And since mankind, according to the witness of Sacred Scripture, was created for eternal life and happiness and since no one is able to attain this eternal life and happiness except through faith in our Lord Jesus Christ, it is necessary to confess that man is of such nature and condition that he is capable of receiving faith in Christ and that everyone who possesses human nature is apt for receiving such faith. Nor is anyone believed to be so foolish that he believes himself capable of attaining that end and by no means capable of attaining the necessary means to that end.

   Therefore the Truth Himself Who can neither deceive nor be

fidei ad officium praedicationis destinaret, dixisse dignoscitur: *euntes docete omnes gentes.* Omnes dixit, absque omni defectu [*delectu*],* cum omnes fidei disciplinae capaces existant. Quod videns et invidens ipsius humani generis aemulus, qui bonis omnibus, ut pereant, semper adversatur, modum excogitavit hactenus inauditum quo impediret, ne verbum Dei gentibus, ut salvae fierent, praedicaretur, ac quosdam suos satellites commovit, qui suam cupiditatem adimplere cupientes, occidentales et meridionales Indos et alias gentes, quae temporibus istis ad nostram notitiam pervenerunt, sub praetextu, quod fidei catholicae expertes existant, uti bruta animalia ad nostra obsequia redigendos esse passim asserere praesumunt. Et eos in servitutem redigunt, tantis afflictionibus illos urgentes quantis vix bruta animalia illis servientia urgeant. Nos igitur, qui ejusdem Domini nostri vices, licet indigni, gerimus in terris, et oves gregis sui nobis commissas, quae extra ejus ovile sunt, ad ipsum ovile toto nisu exquirimus, attendentes Indos

---

* The critical edition of Sublimis found in Parish, as well as the edition of Veritas, uses delectu instead of defectu here (Las Casas in Mexico, 310); the Hernaez text of Veritas does the same (Coleccion, I, 102). In both cases the word should perhaps be defectu.

deceived, when He destined the preachers of the Faith to the office of preaching, is known to have said: "Going, make disciples of all nations." "All," he said, without any exception since all are capable of the discipline of the Faith. Seeing this, and envying it, the enemy of the human race, who always opposes all good men so that the race may perish, has thought up a way, unheard of before now, by which he might impede the saving word of God from being preached to the nations. He has stirred up some of his allies who, desiring to satisfy their own avarice, are presuming to assert far and wide that the Indians of the West and the South who have come to our notice in these times be reduced to our service like brute animals, under the pretext that they are lacking the Catholic Faith. And they reduce them to slavery (*Et eos in servitutem redigunt*), treating them with afflictions they would scarcely use with brute animals. Therefore, We, who, though by no merit of ours, act on earth as the vicar of the same Lord for the sheep of His flock entrusted to us, and who seek with all our strength to bring into the same flock those outside the sheepfold, noting that the Indians themselves indeed are true men and are not only capable of the Christian faith, but, as has

ipsos, utpote, veros homines, non solum Christianae fidei capaces existere, sed, ut nobis innotuit, ad fidem ipsam promptissime currere, ac volentes super his congruis remediis providere, praedictos Indos et omnes alias gentes ad notitiam Christianorum in posterum deventuras, licet extra fidem existant, sua tamen libertate ac rerum suarum domino privatos seu privandos non esse, imo libertate et domino hujusmodi uti, et potiri et gaudere libere et licite posse, nec in servitutem redigi debere: ac quidquid secus fieri contigerit, irritum et inane nulliusque roboris vel momenti, ipsosque Indos et alias gentes verbi Dei praedicatione et exemplo bonae vitae ad dictam fidem Christi invitandos fore. Et praesentius litterarum transumptis manu alicuius Notarii publici subscriptis, ac sigillo alicuius personae in dignitate ecclesiastica constitutae munitis, eadem Fidem adhibendam esse quae originalibus adhiberetur. Auctoritate Apostolica per praesentes decernimus et declaramus, non obstantibus praemissis, coeterisque contrariis quibuscumque. Datum Romae anno 1537, quarto Nonas Junii, Pontificatus nostri anno tertio.

been made known to us, promptly hasten to the faith, and wishing to provide suitable remedies for them, by our Apostolic Authority decree and declare by these present letters that the same Indians and all other peoples — even though they are outside the faith — who shall hereafter come to the knowledge of Christians have not been deprived or should not be deprived of their liberty or of their possessions (*sua libertate ac rerum suarum dominio privatos seu privandos non esse*). Rather they are to be able to use and enjoy this liberty and this ownership of property freely and licitly, and are not to be reduced to slavery (*nec in servitutem redigi debere*), and that whatever happens to the contrary is to be considered null and void and as having no force of law. These same Indians and other peoples are to be invited to the said faith in Christ by preaching and the example of a good life. And We declare that copies of these present letters, signed by the hand of some notary public and having the seal of some person of ecclesiastical rank should carry the same weight as the original. Anything contrary to this decree is null. Given at Rome, June 2, 1537, the third year of our pontificate.

NUMBER THREE:

Paul III: *Veritas Ipsa*, June 2, 1537. Found in *Coleccion de Bulas, Breves y Otros Documentos Relativos a la Iglesia de America y Filipinas*, ed. by El. P. Francisco Javier Hernaez, S.J., Tome I (Bruselas, 1879). Reprinted by Kraus Reprint Ltd. (Vaduz, 1964), pp. 102-03.

Paulus Papa III: Universis Christi fidelibus praesentes litteras inspecturis, salutem et Apostolicam benedictionem.

Veritas ipsa quae nec falli, nec fallere potest, cum Praedictores fidei ad officium praedicationis destinaret, dixisse dignoscitur: *euntes docete omnes gentes.* Omnes dixit, absque omni delectu, cum omnes fidei disciplinae capaces existant. Quod videns et invidens ipsius humani generis aemulus, qui humanis operibus, ut pereant, semper adversatur, modum excogitavit hactenus inauditum quo impediret, ne verbum Dei gentibus, ut salvae fierent, praedicaretur, ac quosdam suos satellites commovit, qui suam cupiditatem adimplere cupientes, occidentales et meridionales Indos et alias gentes, quae temporibus istis ad nostram notitiam pervenerunt, sub praetextu, quod fidei catholicae expertes existant, uti bruta animalia illis servientia urgeant. Nos igitur, qui ejusdem Domini nostri vices, licet indigni, gerimus in terrris, et oves gregis sui nobis commissas, quae extra

Pope Paul III to all the faithful who will read these letters, health and the Apostolic benediction.

The Truth Himself Who can neither deceive nor be deceived, when he destined the preachers of the Faith to the office of preaching, is known to have said: "Going, make disciples of all nations." "All," he said, without any exception since all are capable of the discipline of the Faith. Seeing this, the jealous enemy of the human race, who always works by human means that they may perish, has thought up a way, unheard of before now, by which he might impede the word of God which would keep it from being preached to the nations. He has stirred up some of his allies who, desiring to satisfy their own avarice, are urging that the Indians of the West and the South who have come to our notice in these times be used as servants, like brute animals, under the pretext that they are lacking the Catholic Faith. Therefore, We, who, though unworthy, act on earth as the vicar of the same

ejus ovile sunt, ad ipsum ovile toto nisu exquirimus, attendentes Indos ipsos, utpote, veros homines, non solum Christianae fidei capaces existere, sed, ut nobis innotuit, ad fidem ipsam promptissime currere, ac volentes super his congruis remediis providere, praedictos Indos et omnes alias gentes ad notitiam Christianorum in posterum deventuras, licet extra fidem existant, sua libertate ac rerum suarum domino privatos seu privandos non esse, imo libertate et domino hujusmodi uti, et potiri et gaudere libere et licite posse, nec in servitutem redigi debere: ac quidquid secus fieri contigerit, irritum et inane, ipsosque Indos et alias gentes verbi Dei praedicatione et exemplo bonae vitae ad dictam fidem Christi invitandos fore, authoritate Apostolica per praesentes litteras decernimus, et declaramus, non obstantibus praemissis, coeterisque contrariis quibuscumque. Datum Romae anno 1537, quarto Nonas Junii, Pontificatus nostri anno tertio.

Lord for the sheep of His flock entrusted to us, and who seek with all our strength to bring into the same flock those outside the sheepfold, noting that the Indians themselves indeed are true men and are not only capable of the Christian Faith, but, as has been made known to us, promptly hasten to the faith, and wishing to provide suitable remedies for them, by our Apostolic Authority decree and declare by these present letters that the same Indians and all other peoples — even though they are outside the Faith — who shall hereafter come to the knowledge of Christians have not been deprived or should not be deprived of their liberty or of their possessions (*sua libertate ac rerum suarum dominio privatos seu privandos non esse*). Rather they are to be able to use and enjoy this liberty and this ownership of property freely and licitly, and are not to be reduced to slavery, and that whatever happens to the contrary is to be considered null and void. These same Indians and other peoples are to be invited to the said faith in Christ by preaching and the example of a good life. Anything contrary to this decree is null. Given at Rome, June 2, 1537, the third year of our pontificate.

NUMBER FOUR:

Paul III: Brief *Pastorale Officium* to Cardinal Juan de Tavera of Toledo, May 29, 1537. Found in *Coleccion de Bulas*, pp. 101-02.

Cardinali Toletano etc. — Dilecte fili noster, salutem et Apostolicam benedictionem.

Pastorale officium erga oves nobis coelitus creditas, solerti studio exercentes, sicut earum perditione affligimur, ita promotione laetmur, et non solum illorum bona opera laudamus, sed, ut votivis perfruantur eventibus Apostolicae meditationis curas diffusius interponimus.

Ad nostrum siquidem pervenit auditum, quod carissimus in Christo filius noster Carolus Romanorum Imperator semper Augustus, qui etiam Castellae et Legionis Rex existit, ad reprimendos eos qui cupiditate aestuantes, contra humanum genus inhumanum gerunt animam, publico edicto omnibus sibi subjectis prohibuit, ne quisquam occidentales aut meridionales Indos in servitutem redigere aut eos bonis suis privare praesumat. Nos igitur attendentes Indos ipsos, licet extra gremium Ecclesiae existant, non tamen sua libertate, aut rerum suarum dominio privatos, vel privandos esse, et cum homines ideoque fidei et salutis capaces sint, non servitute delendos, sed praedicationibus, et exemplis ad vitam invitandos fore, ac praeterea Nos talium impiorum tam nefarios ausus reprimere, et ne injuriis, et damnis exasperati, ad

Paul III to Our Beloved Son the Cardinal of Toledo, Health and Apostolic Benediction.

Exercising with proper zeal the Shepherd's office toward the flock divinely entrusted to us, We rejoice with its growth as we are afflicted by its destruction. Not only do we praise their good works, but we also express far and wide the concerns of our Apostolic reflection so that they may enjoy the desired results.

It has come to our attention that our most beloved son the Roman Emperor Charles, also King of Castile and Aragon, has — in order to restrain those who, burning with avarice, deport themselves with an inhuman attitude toward the human race — forbidden by public edict all those subject to him to presume to reduce to slavery (*in servitutem redigere*) any Indians of the West or South or deprive them of their goods. Therefore, attending to the fact that the Indians themselves, although they are outside the bosom of the Church, have not been or should not be deprived of their liberty or of ownership of what is their own and that, since they are men and therefore capable of faith and salvation, they are not

Christi Fidem amplectendam duriores efficiantur, providere cupientes, circumspectioni tuae, de cujus rectitudine, providentia, pietate, et experientia in his, et aliis specialem in Domino fiduciam obtinemus, per praesentes committimus et mandamus, quatenus per te vel alium seu alios praefatis Indis omnibus in praemissis efficacis defensionis praesidio assistens, universis et singulis cujuscumque dignitatis, status, conditionis, gradus, et excellentiae existentibus sub excommunicationis latae sententiae poena, si secus fecerint, ipso facto incurrenda, a qua non nisi a Nobis vel Romano Pontifice pro tempore existente, praeterquam in mortis articulo constituti et satisfactione praevia, absolvi nequeant, districtius inhibeas, ne praefatos Indos quomodolibet in servitutem redigere, aut eos bonis suis spoliare, quoquo modo praesumant, ac contra non parentes ad declarationem incursus excommunicationis hujusmodi ad ulteriora procedas, et alia in praemissis et circa ea necessaria seu quomodolibet opportuna statuas, ordines et disponas, prout prudentiae, probitati et religioni tuae videbitur expedire. Super quibus tibi plenam et liberam facultatem concedimus per praesentes, contrarium facientibus non obstantibus quibuscumque. Datum Romae apud S. Petrum sub annulo Piscatoris dei 29 Maji 1537 Pontificatus nostri anno tertio.

to be given into servitude (*servitute delendos*), but rather by preaching, good example and the like should be invited to [eternal] life, and wishing to repress the evil efforts of such bad men, lest, worn out by injuries and harm, it be more difficult for the Indians to embrace faith in Christ, We place our trust in your vigilance, your rectitude, your providence, your piety and your experience in these and other things and by these letters entrust to you and command that anyone of whatever dignity, state, condition or grade who works against what is done through you or others to help the Indians in the aforementioned matters incurs the penalty of excommunication *latae sententiae*, incurred *ipso facto*. This penalty is to be absolved only by Us or the Roman Pontiff then reigning, except in the case of impending death and with foreseen satisfaction. This is done so that no one in any way may presume to reduce said Indians to slavery (*in servitutem redigere*) or despoil them of their goods. Furthermore, We grant you the right to enact whatever you may additionally decide in your prudence to be necessary to achieve the goals mentioned, anything to the contrary notwithstanding. Given at St. Peter's under the seal of the Fisherman on May 29, 1537, the third year of our pontificate.

NUMBER FIVE:

Pope Gregory XIV: *Cum Sicuti*, April 18, 1591. Found in *Coleccion de Bulas*, p. 108.

Gregorius Papa XIV — Ad perpetuam rei memoriam.

Cum, sicuti nuper accepimus, in primaeva conversione Indorum insularum Philippinarum tanta vitae pericula propter ipsorum Indorum ferocitatem adeunda fuerint, ut multi contra ipsos Indos arma sumere et in bonis damna dare coacti extiterint, ipsique Indis postea, relictis falsis Deorum cultibus, et verum Deum agnoscentes, fidem catholicam amplexi sint, et qui haec damna in bonis ipsorum Indorum dederunt, cupiant bona ablata hujusmodi restituere licet id faciendi facultatem non habeant.

Nos serenitati conscientiarum dictarum personarum consulere, et periculis ac incommodis hujusmodi obviare cupientes, venerabili fratri nostro Episcopo Manilan per praesentes committimus et mandamus, quatenus auctoritate nostra curet ut supradictae personae et domini, quibus facienda est restitutio, inter se desuper componant, ipsique dominis, si certi fuerint, satisfiant: ubi vero certi domini non extiterint, eadem compositio per eumdem Episcopum fiat in utilitatem et subventionem

Pope Gregory XIV: For perpetual remembrance.

As we have recently learned, it happened that when the Philippines were first converted, the Indians were very fierce and many took up arms against them because of the great danger to their own lives. Much harm was done to the Indians in such conflict. Now, since many of the Indians have abandoned their false gods and worship the true God by having embraced the Catholic faith, there are many who realize that the deprivation of the Indians of their goods was wrong, and who wish to make restitution, although they do not have the wherewithal to do so.

Wishing to provide serenity of conscience for the persons mentioned, and desiring to alleviate the dangers and inconvenience involved in this state of affairs, We entrust to the Bishop of Manila the charge of making peace between the people mentioned and their lords, and we order that satisfaction be made to those who are known with certitude to have been injured. When proper owners are not certainly known, let a settlement be arranged by the same bishop that works to the help and

pauperum Indorum, si illi, qui restituere tenentur, id commode facere potuerint, si vero pauperes fuerint, satisfaciant, cum ad meliorem conditionem seu fortunam pervenerint pinguiorem.

Et ne constitutiones et determinationes a dicto Episcopo et Religiosis ac Doctoribus insimul congregatis, ad felicem progressum christianorum noviter ad fidem conversorum factae, ab illis pro suo libito et re vel affectu particulari infringantur; volumus et Apostolica auctoritate decernimus, ut quae ab ipsa Congregatione per suffragia majoris partis in favorem fidei christianae vel salutem animarum, pro bono ipsorum Indorum conversorum regimine ordinata et mandata fuerint, firmiter ac inviolabiliter observentur, donec et quousque ab eadem Congregatione aliter ordinatum vel mandatum fuerit...

Postremo cum, sicut accepimus, carrisimus in Christo filius noster, Philippus, Hispaniarum Rex catholicus, prohibuerit quod nullus Hispanus in praedictis insulis Philippinis mancipia sive servos, etiam jure belli justi et injusti, aut emptionis, vel quovis alio titulo vel praetextu, propter multas fraudes inibi committi solitas, facere vel habere seu retinere audeant, et nonnulli adhuc eadem mancipia, apud se, contra ipsius Philippi Regis edictum vel

advantage of the poor Indians, this settlement to be made by those who are held to such satisfaction. This satisfaction they are to make if they have the means or, of they are now poor themselves, when their own fortunes have improved.

And, lest what is determined by the said bishop — in a Congregation with the religious and learned men — and established for the happy progress of those newly converted to the Faith be infringed by any particular will or desire or event, We ordain and decree by Apostolic authority that the decisions of said congregation made in favor of the Christian faith and the salvation of souls be arrived at by vote of the majority and be firmly and inviolately observed until and when the same congregation shall have determined otherwise...

Furthermore, since, as we have learned, Philip the Catholic King of Spain, our beloved son in Christ, has forbidden that any Spaniard in those Philippine Islands dare to make, have or retain slaves (*mancipia sive servos... facere vel habere seu retinere audeant*), whether by just or unjust war, or through sale or any other title or pretext among the many frauds accustomed to be committed there, and that some do in fact still detain slaves against that edict and mandate of King

mandatum detineant. Nos, ut ipsi Indi ad doctrinas christianas, et ad proprias aedes et bona sua libere et secure absque ullo servitutis metu ire et redire valeant, ut rationi congruit et aequitati; omnibus et singulis, cujuscumque status, gradus, conditionis, ordinis et dignitatis existant, in eisdem insulis existentibus, personis, in virtute sanctae obedientiae et sub excommunicationis poena praecipimus et mandamus, quatenus, publicatis praesentibus, quaecumque mancipia et servos Indos, si quos habent, seu apud se detinent, ac omni dolo et fraude cessante, liberos omnino dimittant et in posterum nec captivos, nec servos ullo modo faciant aut retineant, juxta dicti Philippi Regis edictum seu mandatum...

Datum Romae apud S. Petrum sub annulo Piscatoris die 18 Aprilis 1591, Pontificatus nostri anno primo.

Philip, We — in order that the Indians may go or return to Christian doctrine and their own homes and possessions freely and securely and without any fear of servitude, as befits what is in harmony with reason and justice — decree in virtue of holy obedience and under the penalty of excommunication that if, at the publication of these letters, anyone have or detain such Indians slaves they must give up all craft and deceit, set the slaves completely free and in the future neither make nor retain slaves in any way (*nec servos ullo modo faciant aut retineant*), according to the edict and mandate of said King Philip...

Given at Rome at St. Peter's under the ring of the Fisherman, April 18, 1591, the first year of our pontificate.

NUMBER SIX:

Urban VIII: *Commissum Nobis*, **April 22, 1639. Found in** *Coleccion de Bulas*, **pp. 109-110.**

Dilecto Filio Jurium et Spoliorum Camerae nostrae Apostolicae in Portugalliae et Algarbiorum Regnis debitorum Collectori Generali.

Urbanus Papa VIII. — Dilecte Fili Noster, salutem et Apostlicam benedictionem.

Commissum Nobis a Domino Supremi Apostolatus officii ministerium postulat, ut, nullius hominis salutem a cura nostra alienam ducentes, non solum in Christifideles, sed etiam in eos qui adhuc in ethnicae superstitionis tenebris ex gremio Ecclesiae versantnr, paternae nostrae caritatis affectus diffundamus, et quae eis, quominus ad Christianae veritatis et fidei agnitionem perducantur, quoquomodo obstaculo esse possunt, quantum cum Domino possumus, amovere studeamus.

Alias siquidem fel. rec. Paulus III, Praedecessor Noster, statui Indorum occidentalium et meridionalium, quos in servitutem redigi, suisque bonis privari, eaque de causa ab amplectenda Christi fide averti, acceperat, consulere cupiens; universis et singulis cujuscumque dignitatis, status, conditionis, gradus et dignitatis existentibus, sub excommunicationis latae sententiae poena eo ipso incurrenda, a qua non nisi ab eo vel

To Our Beloved Son, the Collector General of debts for the Apostolic Camera in Portugal.

Pope Urban VIII — to our beloved Son, health and the apostolic blessing.

The ministry of the highest apostolic office, entrusted to us by the Lord, demands that the salvation of no one be outside our concern, not only the salvation of the Christian faithful but also the salvation of those who still exist outside the bosom of the Church in the darkness of native superstition. We pour out the affection of our fatherly charity on them so that they may be led to the knowledge of Christian truth and faith, striving to remove whatever obstacles exist as far as we can with the Lord's help.

At another time our predecessor Paul III desired to take measures in respect to the condition of the Indians of the West and South who were being reduced to slavery (*in servitutem redigi*), deprived of their property and for that reason kept from embracing faith in Christ: he forbade and commanded to be forbidden that said Indians be in any way reduced to slavery (*Indos quomodolibet in servitutem redigere*), or despoiled of their

Romano Pontifice pro tempore existente, praeterquam in mortis articulo et satisfactione praevia, absolvi possent, prohibuit, seu prohiberi mandavit, ne praedictos Indos quomodolibet in servitutem redigere, aut eos bonis suis spoliare quoquomodo praesumerent, et alias prout in ejusdem Pauli Praedecessoris in simili forma Brevis die 29 Maji 1537, desuper expeditis litteris, quarum tenor plenius continetur. Cum autem sicut accepimus causae propter quas Litterae Pauli Pradecessoris praedicti emanarunt, etiam de praesenti vigeant; idcirco Nos ipsius Pauli Praedecessoris vestigiis inhaerendo, ac impiorum hominum ausus, qui Indios praedictos, quos omnibus christianae caritatis et mansuetudinis officiis ad suscipiendam Christi fidem inducere oportet, inhumanitatis actibus ab illa deterrent, reprimere volentes, Tibi per praesentes committimus et mandamus, ut per te vel alium seu alios omnibus Indis, tam in Paraquariae et Brasiliae provinciis ac ad Flumen de la Plata nuncupatae, quam in quibusvis aliis regionibus et locis in Indis occidentalibus et meridionalibus existentibus, in praemissis efficacis defensionis praesidio assistens, universis et singulis personis, tam saecularibus etiam ecclesiasticis, cujuscumque status, sexus, gradus, conditionis et dignitatis, etiam speciali nota et mentione dignis,

property as well as the other things clearly contained in a similar Brief of May 29, 1537 of the same Paul III. He decreed for each and every individual of any dignity, state, condition, or degree who violated his decree the incurring of the penalty of excommunication, *latae sententiae*. He forbade that they be absolved except by himself or by the Roman Pontiff then reigning, except when one was at the point of death and when satisfaction was foreseen. Moreover since we have reason to know that the same causes which prompted the Letters of our Predecessor Paul continue to exist, We ourselves, following the footsteps of Paul our Predecessor and wishing to repress the work of impious men who should induce said Indians to accept faith in Christ by all the means of Christian charity and gentleness but who deter them from it by their inhuman acts, entrust to you the duty and command you by these present letters that, either by yourself or through another or through others that you assist with efficacious defenses all the Indians, both in Paraguay and the provinces of Brazil and along the River Plata, as well as all other Indians living in any other regions and places of the West and South; that you severely prohibit anyone

Appendix B

existentibus, quam cujusvis ordinis, congregationis, societatis, Religionis et instituti, mendicantibus et non mendicantibus, ac Monachal. Regular., sub excommunicationis latae sententiae, per contravenientes eo ipso incurrenda, poena, a qua non nisi a Nobis vel pro tempore existente Romano Pontifice, praeterquam in mortis articulo constituti et satisfactione praevia, absolvi possint, districtius inhibeas, ne de caetero praedictos Indos in servitutem redigere, vendere, emere, commutare, vel donare, ab uxoribus et filiis suis separare, rebus et bonis suis spoliare, ad alia loca deducere et transmittere, aut quoquomode libertate privare, in servitute retinere, necnon praedicta agentibus consilium, auxilium, favorem et operam quocumque praetextu et quaesito colore praestare, aut id licitum praedicare seu docere, ac alios quomodolibet praemissis cooperari audeant seu praesumant. Contradictores quosdam et rebelles, ac Tibi in praemissis non parentes in poenam excommunicationis hujusmodi incidisse declarando, ac per alias etiam censuras et poenas ecclesiasticas, aliaque opportuna juris et facti remedia, appellatione postposita, compescendo etc. — Datum Romae apud S. Petrum sub Annulo Piscatoris die 22 aprilis 1639, pontificatus nostri anno decimo sexto.

from reducing to slavery (*in servitutem redigere*), selling, buying, exchanging, giving away, separating from wives and children, despoiling of their property, taking away to other places, depriving of liberty in any way and keeping in servitude said Indians. This applies as well for all who would give counsel, aid, favor and help of any kind and under any pretext or who preach or teach that such acts are legitimate and all others who dare or presume to cooperate. This injunction applies to each and every person, both secular and ecclesiastic, of whatever state, sex, degree, condition and dignity, even those worthy of special recognition and mention, and to those belonging to any order, congregation, society, religious body, institute, mendicants and non-mendicants, as well as monks and regular clergy. Any of these contravening this decree incur, by that fact, the penalty of excommunication *latae sententiae*, from which no one except We Ourselves or the Roman Pontiff then reigning can absolve except when the person is in danger of death and due satisfaction is foreseen. Etc. — Given at Rome at St. Peter's under the ring of the Fisherman, April 22, 1639, the sixteenth year of our pontificate.

NUMBER SEVEN:

Benedict XIV: *Immensa Pastorum*, **Dec. 20, 1741. Found in Benedict XIV** *Bullarium*, **Tome I (1740-1746), Rome, 1746, Typis Sacrae Congregationis de Propaganda Fide, pp. 99-102.**

Venerabilibus Fratribus, Antistitibus Brasiliae, aliarumque Ditionum Carissimo in Christo Filio Nostro Johanni Portugalliae, et Algarbiorum Regi, in Indiis Occidentalibus, et America subjectarum.

    Venerabiles Fratres, Salutem, et Apostolicam Benedictionem.

    Immensa Pastorum Principis Jesu Christi, qui, ut homines vitam abundantius haberent, venit, et seipsum tradidit redemptionem pro multis, caritas urget Nos, ut, quemadmodum ipsius vices plane immerentes gerimus in terris, ita majorem caritatem non habeamus, quam ut animam nostram, non solum pro Christifidelibus, sed pro omnibus etiam omnino hominibus ponere, satagamus…

    2. Ea propter non sine gravissimo paterni animi nostri maerore accepimus, post tot inita ab iisdem Praedecessoribus Nostris Romanis Pontificibus Apostolicae providentiae consilia, post editas Constitutiones, opem et subsidium ac praesidium Infidelibus omni meliori modo praestandum esse, non injurias, non flagella, non vincula, non servitutem, non necem inferendam

To Our Venerable Brothers, the Bishops of Brazil and other regions of the West Indies and America subject to our beloved Son in Christ, King John of Portugal.

    Venerable Brothers, health and the Apostolic Blessing.

    The immense charity of the Prince of Pastors, Jesus Christ, who came so that men might have life more abundantly and gave himself as redemption for the many, urges us, as we unworthily serve as his vicar on earth, to have no greater charity than to strive to lay down our life not only for Christ's faithful but also for all men whatsoever…

    2. We have received written notice, not without most grave sorrow to our fatherly soul, that, after so much advice of Apostolic providence given by our Predecessors the Roman Pontiffs, after the publication of Constitutions, saying that help, aid, and protection should be given to those who lack faith, and that neither injuries, nor the scourge, nor chains, nor servitude, nor death should be inflicted on them, and all this under the gravest penalties and

esse, sub gravissimis poenis, et Ecclesiasticis censuris, praescribentes; adhuc reperiri, praesertim in istis Brasiliae regionibus, homines Orthodoxae Fidei cultores, qui veluti caritatis, in cordibus nostris per Spiritum Sanctum diffusae sensuum penitus obliti, miseros Indos non solum Fidei luce carentes, verum etiam sacro regenerationis lavacro ablutos, in montanis, asperrimisque earumdem Brasiliae, tam occidentalium, quam meridionalium, aliarumque regionum desertis inhabitantes, aut in servitutem redigere, aut veluti mancipia aliis vendere, aut eos bonis privare, eaque inhumanitate cum iisdem agere praesumant, ut ad amplectenda Christi Fide potissimum avertantur, et ad odio habendam maximopere obfirmentur…

4. Deinde Fraternitates Vestras rogamus atque in Domino hortamur, ut nedum debitam ministerii vestri vigilantiam, sollicitudinem, operamque vestram hac in re, cum nominis dignitatisque vestrae detrimento, deesse non patiamini; quinimmo, studia vestra Regiorum Ministrorum officiis conjungentes, unicuique probetis, Sacerdotes, animarum pastores quanto prae Laicis Ministris, ad Indis hujusmodi opem ferendam, eosque ad Catholicam Fidem adducendos,

censures of the Church, there are still found, especially in the regions of Brazil, members of the True Faith who, completely oblivious, as it were, of the charity poured out in our hearts by the Holy Spirit, presume to deal with the unfortunate Indians who dwell in the harsh mountain regions of the same Brazil, whether north or south or in other deserted regions — not only those who lack the Faith, but even those cleansed by the washing of regeneration — by reducing them to slavery (*redigere servitutem*), or selling them to others as if they were property (*aut veluti mancipia aliis vendere*), or depriving them of their goods, or dealing with them inhumanly, so that they are strongly turned from embracing faith in Christ and are greatly confirmed in a hatred for it…

4. And so we ask and exhort you, Brothers, that in this matter you permit no lack in the vigilance, solicitude and work due your ministry, to the detriment of your names and dignity; rather, burning with the ardent zeal of priestly charity, join your efforts to the rulers of the regions so that priests and laity bring help to these Indians and lead them to the Catholic faith.

5. Furthermore, we, by Apostolic authority, and holding to the same course, renew and confirm

ardentiori Sacerdotalis caritatis aestu ferveant.

5. Praeterea Nos, auctoritate Apostolica, tenore praesentium, Apostolicas in simili forma Brevis Literas a fel. rec. Paulo Papa III Praedecessore nostro, ad tunc existentem Johannem Sanctae Romanae Ecclesiae Cardinalem de Tavera nuncupatum Archiepiscopum Toletanum die 28 mensis Maji anno 1537 datas, et a rec. mem. Urbano Papa VIII itidem Praedecessore nostro, tunc existenti jurium et spoliorum Camerae Apostolicae in Portugalliae et Algarbiorum Regnis debitorum Collectori Generali, die 22 mensis Aprilis anno 1639, scriptas renovamus, et confimamus; necnon eorumdem Pauli, et Urbani Praedecessorum vestigiis inhaerendo, ac impiorum hominum ausus, qui Indos praedictos, quos omnibus Christianae Caritatis et mansuetudinis officiis ad suscipiendam Christi Fidem inducere oportet, inhumanitatis actibus ab illa deterrent, reprimere, volentes, unicuique Fraternitatum vestrarum, vestrisque pro tempore Successoribus committimus et mandamus, ut unusquisque vestrum, vel per se ipsum, vel per alium, seu alios, editis atque in publicum propositis affixisque edictis, omnibus Indis, tam in Paraquariae et Brasiliae Provinciis,

the Apostolic Letters in the form of a Brief written by our Predecessor Pope Paul III to John of Tavera, then Cardinal of the Holy Roman Church and Archbishop of Toledo on May 28, 1537, and by our Predecessor Urban VIII to the then Collector General of Debts of the Apostolic Camera in Portugal on April 22, 1639; following in the footsteps of the same Paul and Urban our Predecessors, and wishing to repress the daring of impious men who should lead all by Christian charity and mildness to accept faith in Christ but who deter said Indians from it by inhuman actions, We entrust to each of you and your successors and We command that, either by yourself or by someone or some others — when these letters have been published — that you efficaciously assist said Indians, both in Paraguay and the Provinces of Brazil and along the River Plata and in all other regions and places in the Indies, and let it be known that each and every person, both secular and ecclesiastic of whatever status, sex, grade, condition and dignity, even those worthy of special note and dignity, of any Order, Congregation, Society (even the Society of Jesus), Religion, Mendicant and non-Mendicant, monks, Regulars, as well as the Military Brotherhood, even the Hospitalers of St.

ac ad Flumen de la Plata nuncupatum, quam in quibusvis aliis regionibus, et locis in Indiis occidentalibus et Meridionalibus, existentibus, in praemissis efficacis defensionis praesidio assistentes, universis et singulis personis, tam saecularibus, etiam Ecclesiasticis cujuscumque status, sexus, gradus, conditionis, et dignitatis, etiam speciali nota, et mentione dignis existentibus, quam cujusvis Ordinis, Congregationis, Societatis, etiam Jesu, Religionis et Instituti, Mendicantium, et non Mendicantium, ac Monachalis, Regularibus, etiam quarumcumque Militiarum, etiam Hospitalis Sancti Johannis Hierosolymitani, Fratribus Militibus, sub excommunicationis latae sententiae per Contravenientes eo ipso incurrenda poena, a qua, nonnisi a Nobis, vel pro tempore existente Romano Pontifice, praeterquam in mortis articulo constituti, et satisfactione praevia, absolvi possint, districtius inhibeant; ne de coetero praedictos Indos in servitutem redigere, vendere, emere, commutare, vel donare, ab Uxoribus, et Filiis suis separare, rebus et bonis suis spoliare, ad alia loca deducere et transmittere, aut quoquo modo libertate privare, in servitute retinere; necnon praedicta

John of Jerusalem, who contravenes these edicts will incur, *eo ipso*, excommunication *latae sententiae*. From this excommunication they can be absolved only by us or by the Roman Pontiff then existing, except in the case of being at the point of death, and having made satisfaction; those incur this penalty who reduce said Indians to slavery (*praedictos Indos in servitutem redigere*), sell them, buy them, exchange them or give them away, separate them from their wives and children, despoil them of their property and goods, lead or transmit them to other places, or in any manner deprive them of liberty to retain them in servitude; as well as those who offer counsel, aid or favor to those who do such things; We declare that anyone who contradicts or rebels against these things or does not agree with you in respect to said matters falls under penalty of this excommunication as well as under any other ecclesiastical censures and penalties and other opportune remedies... We grant and bestow on each of you and your successors the full and free power of doing this, as well as the right to call upon the secular authorities, if there is need, in case of repeated violations.

6. All things to the contrary notwithstanding...

agentibus consilium, auxilium, favorem, et operam quocumque praetextu, et quaesito colore praestare, aut id licitum praedicare, seu docere, ac alias quomodolibet praemissis cooperari audeant, seu praesumant; Contradictores quoslibet et rebelles, ac unicuique Vestrum in praemissis non parentes, in poenam excommunicationis hujusmodi incidisse declarando, ac per alias etiam censuras et poenas Ecclesiasticas, aliaque opportuna juris, et facti remedia, appellatione postposita, compescendo legitimisque super his habendis servatis processibus, censuras et poenas ipsas etiam iteratis vicibus aggravando, invocato etiam ad hoc, si opus fuerit, auxilio brachii saecularis. Nos enim unicuique Vestrum, vestrorumque pro tempore Successorum, desuper plenam, amplam et liberam facultatem tribuimus, et impertimur.

6. Non obstantibus, etc ...

Datum Romae apud S. Mariam Majorem sub Annulo Piscatoris die 20 Decembris 1741.
Pontificatus Nostri Anno Secundo.

Given at Rome at St. Mary Major, under the seal of the Fisherman, on December 20, 1741, the second year of our pontificate.

NUMBER EIGHT:

Gregory XVI: *In Supremo*, December 3, 1839. Found in *Coleccion de Bulas*, pp. 114-116.

Gregorius Papa XVI. — Ad futuram rei memoriam.

In supremo Apostolatus fastigio constituti, et, nullis licet suffragantibus meritis, gerentes vicem Jesu Christi Dei Filii, qui propter nimiam caritatem suam Homo factus, mori etiam pro mundi redemptione dignatus est, ad Nostram pastoralem sollicitudinem pertinere animadvertimus, ut fideles ab inhumano Nigritarum seu aliorum quorumcumque hominum mercatu avertere, penitus studeamus. Sane cum primum diffundi coepit Evangelii lux, senserunt alleviari plurimum apud christianos conditionem suam miseri illi, qui tanto tunc numero, bellorum praesertim occasione, in servitutem durissimam deveniebant. Inspirati enim a divino spiritu Apostoli servos quidem ipsos docebant obedire dominis carnalibus sicut Christo, et facere voluntatem Dei ex animo; dominis vero praecipiebant, ut bene erga servos agerent, et quod justurm est et aequum eis praestarent, ac remitterent minas, scientes quia illorum et ipsorum Dominus est in coelis et personarum acceptio non

Pope Gregory XVI: For perpetual memory.

Since, through no merits of our own, We have been placed at the highest point of the Apostolate as Vicar of Jesus Christ the Son of God, Who because of His great charity willed to become man and die for the redemption of the world, We consider it to belong to our pastoral solicitude to avert the faithful from the inhuman trade in Negroes and all other groups of humans. Surely, since the light of the Gospel was first spread abroad, those unfortunate people who in such great numbers, and due especially to war had fallen into very cruel slavery, have experienced some relief especially when they were among Christians. Inspired by the Divine Spirit, the Apostles indeed urged slaves themselves to obey their masters according to the flesh as though obeying Christ, and to do the Will of God from their heart. However, the Apostles ordered the masters to act well towards their slaves, to give them what was just and equitable, and to refrain from threats, knowing that the Lord in heaven, with Whom there is no partiality in respect to

est apud Eum. Universim vero cum sincera erga omnes caritas Evangelii lege summopere commendaretur, et Christus Dominus declarasset habiturum se tamquam factum aut denegatum sibi ipsi quidquid benignitatis et misericordiae minimis et indigentibus praestitum aut negatum fuisset, facile inde contigit, nedum christiani servos suos praesertim christianos, veluti fratrum loco haberent, sed etiam ut proniores essent ad illos, qui mererentur, libertate donandos; quod quidem occasione in primis Paschalium solemnium fieri consuevisse indicat Gregorius Nyssenus. Nec defuerunt qui, ardentiore caritate excitati, se ipsos in vincula conjecerunt, ut alios redimerent; quorum multos se novisse testatur Apostolicus vir, idemque sanctissimae recordationis, praedecessor Noster Clemens I. Igitur progressu temporis, ethnicarum superstitionum caligine plenius dissipata, et rudiorum quoque populorum moribus, fidei per caritatem operantis beneficio, mitigatis, res eo tandem devenit, ut jam a pluribus saeculis nulli apud plurimas christianorum gentes servi habeantur. Verum dolentes admodum dicimus, fuerunt subinde ex ipso fidelium numero, qui sordidioris lucri cupidine turpiter obcaecati, in

persons, is indeed Lord of the slaves and of themselves. Indeed, since a sincere charity towards all was commended by the law of the Gospel, and since Our Lord Jesus Christ had declared that He considered as done or refused to Himself everything kind and merciful done or refused to the small and needy, it readily follows not only that Christians should regard as brothers their slaves, especially their Christian slaves, but that they should be more inclined to set free those who deserve it. Indeed this was the custom especially upon the occasion of the Easter Feast as Gregory of Nyssa tells us. Nor were there lacking Christians, who, moved by an ardent charity delivered themselves into captivity in order to redeem others. That Apostolic man, our predecessor of holy memory, Clement I, testified that he himself knew many instances of this. Therefore, in the course of time, when the darkness of pagan superstition was more fully dissipated and the customs of the uneducated people had been mitigated due to Faith operating by charity, it at last came about that, for several centuries now, there have been no slaves in the greater number of Christian peoples. But, We still say it with sorrow, there were to be found

dissitis remotisque terris Indos, Nigritas, miserosve alios in servitutem redigere, seu instituto ampliatoque commercio eorum, qui captivi facti ab aliis fuerant, indignum horum facinus juvare non dubitarent. Haud sane praetermiserunt plures gloriosae memoriae Romani Pontifices, praedecessores Nostri, reprehendere graviter pro suo munere illorum rationem, utpote spirituali ipsorum saluti noxiam et christiano nomini probrosam; ex qua etiam illud consequi pervidebant, ut infidelium gentes ad veram nostram religionem odio habendam magis magisque obfirmarentur. Quo spectant Apostolicae litterae Pauli III die 13 Maji 1537 [sic*] sub Piscatoris annulo datae ad Cardinalem Archiepiscopum Toletanum: et aliae deinceps eisdem ampliores ab Urbano VIII datae die 22 Aprilis 1639 ad Collectorem Jurium Camerae Apostolicae in Portugallia, quibus in litteris ii nominatim gravissime coercentur, qui Occidentales vel Meridionales Indos in servitutem redigere, vendere, emere, commutare vel donare, ab uxoribus et filiis suis separare, rebus et bonis suis spoliare, ad alia loca deducere et transmittere, aut quoquomodo libertate privare, in servitute retinere, nec non praedicta agentibus consilium, auxilium,

subsequently among the faithful some who, shamefully blinded by the desire of sordid gain, in lonely and distant countries, did not hesitate to reduce to slavery (*in servitutem redigere*) Indians, Blacks and other unfortunate peoples, or else, by instituting or expanding the trade in those who had been made slaves by others, aided the crime of others. Certainly many Roman Pontiffs of glorious memory, Our Predecessors, did not fail, according to the duties of their office, to blame severely this way of acting as dangerous for the spiritual welfare of those who did such things and a shame to the Christian name. They foresaw that it would follow from such activity that the peoples who did not have the Faith would be more and more confirmed in their hatred of the true Religion. It is to these practices that the Apostolic Letters of Paul III, given on May 29, 1537, under the seal of the Fisherman, and addressed to the Cardinal Archbishop of Toledo, and afterwards another more detailed Letter was addressed by Urban VIII on April 22, 1639 to the Collector of Laws of the Apostolic Chamber of Portugal. In the latter are severely and particularly condemned those who would dare to reduce to slavery (*in servitutem redigere*) the Indians of the Western and Southern Indies,

favorem et operam quocumque praetextu et quaesito colore praestare, aut id licitum praedicare seu docere, aut alias quomodolibet praemissis cooperari auderent, seu prae sumerent.

Has memoratorum Pontificum sanctiones confirmavit postmodum et renovavit Benedictus XIV novis apostolicis litteris ad Antistites Brasiliae et aliarum quarumdam regionum datis die 20 Decembris 1741, quibus eumdem in finem ipsorum praesulum sollicitudinem excitavit. Antea quoque alius his antiquior Praedecessor Noster, Pius II, cum sua aetate Lusitanorum imperium in Guineam, Nigritarum regionem, proferretur, litteras dedit die 7 Octobris 1462 ad Episcopum Rubicensem eo profecturum: in quibus nedum Antistiti ipsi opportunas ad sacrum ministerium inibi cum majori fructu exercendum, facultates impertitus fuit, sed eadem occasione graviter in christianos illos animadvertit, qui Neophytos in servitutem abstrahebant. Et nostris etiam temporibus Pius VII eodem, qui sui Decessoris, religionis et caritatis spiritu inductus, officia sua apud potentes viros sedulo interposuit, ut Nigritarum commercium tandem inter christianos omnino cessaret.

sell them, buy them, exchange them or give them away, separate them from their wives and children, despoil them of their property, conduct or transport them into other regions, or deprive them of liberty in any way whatsoever, retain them in servitute, or lend counsel, aid, favor and help to those acting this way, no matter what the pretense or excuse. Likewise reprobated is anyone who proclaims and teaches that this way of acting is permissible and who co-operates in any manner whatever in the practices mentioned.

Benedict XIV afterwards confirmed and renewed the sanctions of the said Popes in new Apostolic Letters addressed on December 20, 1741, to the Bishops of Brazil and some other regions, in which he encouraged, to the same end, the solicitude of the rulers themselves. Pius II, another of Our Predecessors, who lived before Benedict XIV, since during his life the power of the Portuguese was extending itself over Guinea, sent on October 7, 1462, to the Bishop of Rubicon who was setting out for that country, letters in which he not only gives to the bishop himself the means of exercising there the sacred ministry more fruitfully, but on the same occasion, takes grave notice of those Christians who were reducing neophytes to slavery (*in*

Hae quidem Praedecessorum Nostrorum sanctiones et curae profuerunt, Deo bene juvante, non parum Indis aliisque praedictis a crudelitate invadentium, seu a mercatorum christianorum cupiditate tutandis: non ita tamen ut sancta haec sedes de pleno suorum in id studiorum exitu laetari posset: quum imo commercium Nigritarum, etsi nonnulla ex parte imminutum, adhuc tamen a christianis pluribus exerceatur. Quare Nos, tantum hujusmodi probrum a cunctis christianorurm finibus avertere cupientes, ac re universa nonnullis etiam venerabilibus Fratribus Nostris S.R.E. Cardinalibus in consilium adhibitis, mature perpensa, Praedecessorum Nostrorum insistentes vestigiis, auctoritate Apostolica, omnes cujuscumque conditionis Christi fideles admonemus et obtestamur in Domino vehementer, ne quis audeat in posterum Indos, Nigritas, seu alios hujusmodi homines injuste vexare, aut spoliare suis bonis, aut in servitutem redigere, vel aliis talia in eos patrantibus auxilium aut favorem praestare, seu exercere inhumanum illud commercium, quo Nigritae, tanquam si non homines, sed pura, putaque animantia forent, in servitutem utcumque redacti, sine ullo discrimine contra justitiae et *servitutem abstrahebant).* In our time Pius VII, moved by the same religious and charitable spirit as his Predecessors, dutifully used his good offices with those in power to end completely the slave trade at least among Christians. Indeed these sanctions and this concern of Our Predecessors availed in no small measure, with the help of God, to protect the Indians and the other peoples mentioned from the cruelties of the invaders and from the greed of Christian traders: it was not such, however, that the Holy See could rejoice over the complete success of its efforts in this matter. The slave trade, although it has been somewhat diminished, is still carried on by numerous Christians. Therefore, desiring to remove such a great shame from all Christian peoples, having fully reflected on the whole question, having taken the advice of many of Our Venerable Brothers the Cardinals of the holy Roman Church, and walking in the footsteps of Our Predecessors, We, by apostolic authority, warn and strongly exhort in the Lord faithful Christians of every condition that no one in the future dare to bother unjustly, despoil of their possessions, or reduce to slavery (*in servitutem redigere*) Indians, Blacks or other such peoples. Nor are they to lend aid and favor to those who give themselves up to these

humanitatis jura emuntur, venduntur, ac durissimis interdum laboribus exantlandis devoventur, et insuper lucri spe, primis Nigritarum occupantoribus per commercium idem proposita, dissidia etiam et perpetua quodammodo in illorum regionibus praelia foventur.

Enimvero Nos praedicta omnia, tamquam christiano nomini prorsus indigna, auctoritate Apostolica reprobamus; eademque auctoritate districte prohibemus atque interdicimus, ne quis ecclesiasticus vel laicus ipsum illud Nigritarum commercium, veluti licitum sub quovis obtentu aut quaesito colore tueri aut aliter contra ea, quae nostris hisce Apostolicis litteris monuimus, praedicare, seu quomodolibet publice vel privatim docere praesumat.

Ut autem eaedem hae Nostrae litterae omnibus facilius innotescant, nec quisquam illarum ignorantiam allegare possit, decernimus et mandamus illas ad valvas Basilicae... publicari...

Datum Romae apud S. Mariam Majorem sub annulo Piscatoris die 3 Decembris 1839, pontificatus nostri anno nono.

practices, or exercise that inhuman traffic by which the Blacks, as if they were not humans but rather mere animals, having been brought into slavery in no matter what way, are, without any distinction and contrary to the rights of justice and humanity, bought, sold and sometimes given over to the hardest labor, to which is added the fact that in the hope of gain, proposed by the first owners of the Blacks for this same trade, dissensions and almost perpetual conflicts have arisen in those regions.

We then, by Apostolic Authority, condemn all such practices as absolutely unworthy of the Christian name. By the same Authority We prohibit and strictly forbid any Ecclesiastic or lay person from presuming to defend as permissible this trade in Blacks under no matter what pretext or excuse, or from publishing or teaching in any manner whatsoever, in public or privately, opinions contrary to what We have set forth in these Apostolic Letters.

Moreover so that these letters may be known more easily by all, lest anyone pretend ignorance of them, We decree and order that they be published on the walls of the Basilica...

Given at Rome at St. Mary Major, under the seal of the Fisherman on Dec. 3, 1839, the ninth year of our pontificate.

APPENDIX C

Instructions of the Holy Office on Slavery

NUMBER ONE:

Instruction Number 230: Found in *Collectanea S. Congregationis de Propaganda Fide seu Decreta Instructiones Rescripta pro Apostolicis Missionibus* (Rome: Polygot Press, 1907), Vol. I, pp. 76-77.

S.C.S. Officii 20 Martii 1686
Propositiones:
1. Licitum est nigros aliosque sylvestres nemini infensos vi aut dolo captivare.
2. Licet nigros aliosque sylvestres, nemini infensos, vi aut dolo captivatos emere, vendere, et de illis alios contractus facere.
3. Cum nigri aliique sylvestres, iniuste captivati, sunt permixti aliis iuste vendibilibus, licet omnes emere, sive, ut dicunt, bonos et malos.
4. Emptores nigrorum aliorumve sylvestrium non tenentur inquirere de titulo eorum servitutis, sintne iuste vel iniuste, mancipia, licet sciant plurimos eorum esse iniuste captivatos.
5. Possessores nigrorum aliorumve sylvestrium nemini infensorum, vi aut dolo captorum, ad eos manumittendos non tenentur.
6. Captores nigrorum et aliorum sylvestrium, nemini

Congregation of the Holy Office: Response of March 20, 1686
It is asked:
1. Whether it is permitted to capture by force or deceit Blacks (*nigros*) or other natives (*sylvestres*) who have harmed no one.
2. Whether it is permitted to buy, sell or make other contracts in their respect Blacks or other natives (*sylvestres*) who have harmed no one and been made captives by force or deceit.
3. Whether it is permitted to buy Blacks or other natives, unjustly captured and who are now mixed among other salable goods.
4. Whether buyers of Blacks and other natives are not held to inquire about their title of servitude, viz. whether they have justly or unjustly been enslaved (*sintne iuste vel iniuste*), even when they know that very many of them have been unjustly captured.

infensorum, vi aut dolo captorum, emptores, possessores, non tenentur ad eorum damna compensanda.

7-11 ...

R. Ad. 1,2, et 3: Non licere.
Ad. 4, 5 et 6. Tenentur.

5. Whether the possessors of Blacks and other natives who have harmed no one and been captured by force or deceit, are not held to set them free.

6. Whether the captors, buyers and possessors of Blacks and other natives who have harmed no one and who have been captured by force or deceit are not held to make compensation to them.

7-11 ...

Response:

To numbers 1,2,3: it is not permitted.

To numbers 4, 5 and 6: they are obliged.

Appendix C

NUMBER TWO:

Instruction Number 515: Found in *Collectanea*, Vol I, p. 316.

S.C.S. Officii 12 Sept. 1776. Cocincin.

Ab aevo cambodienses christiani in sui famulatum emunt laossenses aliosque ex populis confinibus, idque agunt etiamsi dubium fundatum sit, immo etiamsi aliquando certo sciant, quod illa mancipia fuerint in patria sua furto ablata.

R. *Instructio Pii PP. VI*: In primis distinguendum est, num captivi laossenses qui a plagiariis veneunt, sublati fuerint *legitimo eorum domino*, vel potius liberi ac proprii iuris in plagiariorum iniustam servitutem devenerint. In primo casu non licet eos emere; etsi enim iniuste a plagiariis detineantur, nefas tamen est alienas res furto ablatas emere invito domino. In secundo casu iterum pariter distinguendum est, num laossenses se christianis venum ire detrectent, vel consentiant: si detrectant, emi nequamquam possunt, ipsi enim captivi domini sunt propriae libertatis, quamvis iniuste iis per furtum a plagiariis ereptae. Si vero postquam plene edocti fuerint iure sibi libertatem competere, a qua nonnisi aliorum iniuria exciderunt, ultro et sponte sua, et ex libera et propria voluntate, tamquam rerum suarum

Sacred Congregation of the Holy Office, Sept. 12, 1776. To Indochina.

For a very long time Christian Cambodians have purchased into their service Laotians and other neighboring people, and they do this even though there be a founded doubt — and even if they sometimes certainly know — that these servants were taken by theft from their own country.

Response: *Instruction of Pope Pius VI*: In the first place one must distinguish whether the captive Laotians who are sold by kidnappers have been taken from *their legitimate owners*, or rather whether, free and of their own right, have come into the unjust slavery of the kidnappers. In the first case it is not permitted to buy them; even if they be unjustly detained by kidnappers, it is nevertheless wrong to buy what has been taken from another by theft, against the will of the owner. In the second case, one must also make a distinction, namely whether the Laotians decline to be sold to Christians, or consent to it: if they decline, they are by no means able to be purchased for these captives are masters of their own freedom although it has been unjustly snatched from them by kidnappers.

domini, se exhibeant christianis *ut ab eis recipiantur et detineantur in servitutem* eo prudenti consilio ut a graviori et dura plagiariorum servitute soluti, a qua ipsis datum non fuerit alio modo se emancipare, mitiorem apud emptores christianos servitutem sortiantur, penes quos etiam facile sibi persuadere poterunt, venire posse in agnitionem veri Dei cultus, eumque inaestimabili animarum suarum compendio profiteri; in his sane circumstantiis permitti poterit christianis, habito etiam respectu ad favorem fidei, ut possint eiusmodi captivos iusto pretio sibi comparare, et *in propriam servitutem redigere et retinere*, dummodo eo animo sint, ut eos tractent secundum praecepta caritatis christianae, et curent etiam rudimentis fidei illos imbuere, adeo ut, si fieri poterit, in libertatem filiorum Dei, quae in sola Catholica Ecclesia est, nulla tamen coactione facta, sed tantummodo opportunis suasionibus et hortationibus, libere et feliciter traducantur per eorum conversionem ad veram fidem.

If indeed, after they have been fully taught that freedom belongs to them by right and which they lose only by injury to others, they spontaneously and by their own free will, as masters of themselves, present themselves to Christians to be received by them and held in servitude, by a prudent plan in order to be freed from the more grave and harsh servitude to the kidnappers, from which they have in no way the ability to free themselves, and choose a milder servitude in the hands of Christian buyers and with whom they are easily able to persuade themselves that they can come to a knowledge of worshipping the true God, and of confessing Him to the inestimable advantage of their souls; in such circumstances it is permissible for the Christians, especially when they act in favor of the Faith, to purchase such captives for a just price, and *to take and retain them in their own servitude*, as long as they are of the mind to treat them according to the precepts of Christian charity, and take care to imbue them with the rudiments of the Faith so that, if it is possible, they may be freely and happily led, this being done by no compulsion, but only by opportune persuasion and encouragement, through their conversion to the True Faith into the liberty of the sons of God which is found only in the Catholic Church.

NUMBER THREE:

Instruction Number 1293: Found in *Collectanea*, Vol. I, pp. 715-720.

Instr. S.C.S. Off. 20 Iunii 1866
Pro Vic. Ap. Ad. Gallas.
Delata sunt ad hanc S.C. Supremae Inquisitionis plurima dubia quae proposuit R.P.D. Guillelmus Massaia Vicarius Apostolicus apud Gallas in Africa, quaeque in octo diversas classes distingui commode possunt. Prima classis respicit polygamiam simultaneam tam ex parte viri, quam ex parte uxorum; altera modum quo filiaefamilias nuptui traduntur; tertia baptismum eorum qui perversionis periculo praevidentur obnoxii; quarta emptionem, venditionem, fugam, coercitionem, matrimonia servorum; quinta inimicitias, communis vindictae nomine, inter gallarum independentium tribus exerceri solitas;...

IV. Quarta dubiorum classis, de servorum emptione et venditione. Servitutis proprie a dictae conditio apud Gallas et Sydamas tam stricte cohaeret cum sociali eorum statu, ut impossibile fere sit domum inter eos sine mancipiis figere et retinere. Illic enim reperire non est servos conducticios, et quilibet paterfamilias omnia prosus sibi suaeque domui comparare debet, sive quae e terra gignuntur, sive

Instruction of the Sacred Congregation of the Holy Office, June 20, 1866.

For the Vicar Apostolic among the Galla.

There have been sent to this Sacred Congregation of the Inquisition many questions proposed by the Rev. William Massaia, Vicar Apostolic among the Galla in Africa. For convenience these questions can be broken up into eight different kinds. The first kind deals with simultaneous polygamy both on the part of the man and the part of the wife; the second touches on the manner in which the daughters of a family are given in marriage; the third touches on the baptism of those for whom a danger of loss of faith is foreseen; the fourth touches on the buying, selling, flight, punishment and marriage of slaves; the fifth touches on the enmities or feuds exercised among the independent tribes of the Galla,...

IV. The fourth type of question concerns the buying and selling of slaves. "The condition of servitude, properly so called, among the Galla and Sidama so strictly coheres with their social status that

quae hominum industria fiunt. Praeterea mancipia habentur veluti principalis commercii materia, immo valent quadamtenus pro numerata pecunia, eademque saepe ad solutionem debiti vel principis iussu, vel legum ipsarum praescripto creditores acce ptare tenentur. Quae cum ita se habeant, quaeritur:

"12. An liceat christianis apud Gallas et Sidamas mancipia emere, et in debiti solutionem, aut in donum recipere, quotiescumque id agant propter domus vel familiae suae necessitates, sine animo eadem mancipia revendendi.

"13. An familia aliqua christiana non lucri faciendi consilio, sed tantum ob gravem victus comparandi, vel debitorum solvendorum necessitatem, possit licite aut tradere in pretium, aut vendere servum quem possidet.

"14. An liceat admittere ad sacramentorum participationem christianum quemdam negotiatorem, qui a servis quaestus causa emendis et vendendis abhorrere quidem solet, sed ne detrimentum rei familiaris patiatur, servos aliquos revendere vult, quos olim nobilium emptorum praepotentia recipere coactus est pro mercium suarum pretio.

"15. An christiani, ipsique

it is almost impossible to establish and maintain a home among them without the buying of slaves. Because of this it is not found that servants are hired, and every head of a household has to buy completely everything for himself and for his household, be they things grown from the land or made by human industry. Therefore the slaves are held like a principal matter of commerce; in a certain degree they have the value of money, and frequently, by the order of the leader or by prescript of their laws, creditors are held to accept them for the payment of debt. All this being the case, I ask:

"12. Whether it is permitted for Christians among the Galla and Sidama to buy slaves, or to receive them as payment for a debt or as a gift as long as they act for the sake of the necessities of their home and family and without the intention of re-selling the slaves.

"13. Whether a Christian family, not for the sake of gain, but only because of a grave means of support or the necessity of paying a debt is permitted to trade or sell a slave it possesses.

"14. Whether it is permitted to admit to the sacraments any Christian merchant who normally abhors the buying and selling of slaves for the sake of profit, but, lest he suffer harm to his family

adeo missionarii licite possint interesse tamquam testes, vel sequestres, vel alio nomine contractibus, iudiciis, aut aliis id genus publicis actibus, qui secundum gentium illarum leges fiunt circa servos.

Etsi Romani Pontifices nihil intentatum re liquerint quo servitutem ubique gentium abolerent, iisdemque praecipue acceptum referri debeat quod iam a pluribus saeculis nulli apud plurimas christianorum gentes servi habeantur; tamen servitus ipsa per se et absolute considerata iuri naturali et divino minime repugnat, pluresque adesse possunt iusti servitutis tituli quos videre est apud probatos theologos sacrorumque canonum interpretes. Dominium enim illud, quod domino in servum competit non aliud esse intelligitur quam ius perpetuum de servi operis in proprium commodum disponendi, quas quidem homini ab homine praestari fas est. Inde autem consequitur iuri naturali et divino non repugnare quod servus vendatur, ematur, commutetur, donetur, modo in hac venditione, emptione, commutatione, donatione, debitae conditiones accurate serventur quas itidem probati auctores late perse quuntur et explicant. Quas inter conditiones illa praecipuum sibi vindicat locum, ut emptor

affairs, wants to resell some slaves whom once he was forced, by a seller who was a noble, to take as the price for his wages.

"15. Whether Christians and even missionaries can licitly be present as witnesses or agents or other such name at contracts, judgments or other types of public acts which deal with slaves according to the laws of those peoples."

[Response] Although the Roman Pontiffs have left nothing untried by which servitude be everywhere abolished among the nations, and although it is especially due to them that already for many ages no slaves are held among very many Christian peoples, nevertheless, servitude itself, considered in itself and all alone (*per se et absolute*), is by no means repugnant to the natural and divine law, and there can be present very many just titles for servitude, as can be seen by consulting the approved theologians and interpreters of the canons. For the dominion which belongs to a master in respect to a slave is not to be understood as any other than the perpetual right of disposing, to one's own advantage, of servile work, which dominion it is legitimate for a person to offer to another person. From this it follows that it is not repugnant to

diligenter examinet, num servus qui venum exponitur iuste an iniuste libertate sua privatus fuerit, et venditor nihil committat, quo servi ad alium possessorem transferendi vita, honestas, aut catholica fides in discrimen adducatur. Christiani igitur, de quibus in dubio primo sermo fit, licite possunt servos emere atque in debiti solutionem, vel in donum recipere, quoties moraliter certi sint servos illos neque legitimo eorum domino sublatos, neque iniuste in servitutem fuisse abstractos. Si enim servi qui ad emendum offeruntur, legitimo eorum domino ablati fuerunt, non licet eos emere, quia nefas est alienas res furto ablatas emere invito domino. Si autem iniuste in servitutem redacti fuerint, distinguendum est num se christianis venum ire aut donari detrectent, vel consentiant. Si detrectant, emi aut recipi nequa quam possunt, ipsi enim captivi domini sunt propriae libertatis, quamvis iniuste iis ereptae. Si vero postquam plene edocti fuerint iure sibi libertatem competere, a qua nonnisi aliorum iniuria exciderunt, ultro et sponte sua, et ex libera et propria voluntate tamquam rerum suarum domini se exhibeant christianis ut ab eis recipiantur et detineantur in servitutem, eo prudenti consilio ut a dura servitute praesenti, a qua

the natural and divine law that a slave be sold, bought, exchanged, or given, as long as in this sale, or buying, or exchange or giving, the due conditions which those same approved authors widely follow and explain, are properly observed. Among these conditions those which are to be especially looked at are whether the slave who is put up for sale has been justly or unjustly deprived of his liberty, and that the seller does nothing by which the slave to be transferred to another possessor suffer any detriment to life, morals or the Catholic faith. Therefore, Christians, about whom one is speaking in the first question, can licitly buy slaves or, to resolve a debt, receive them as a gift, as long as they are morally certain that those slaves were not taken from their legitimate master or reduced to slavery unjustly. For if the slaves who are offered for sale have been taken from their legitimate master, it is not permitted to buy them, because it is a crime to buy what belongs to another and has been taken, the master being unwilling, by theft. If, however, they have been unjustly reduced to slavery, then one must determine whether they are unwilling to be sold or given to Christians or whether they consent to it. If they are unwilling, they can by no means be

ipsis datum non fuerit alio modo se emancipare, mitiorem apud dominos christianos servitutem sortiantur, penes quos etiam facile sibi persuadere poterunt, venire posse in cognitionem veri Dei cultus, eumque inaestimabili animarum suarum compendio profiteri, in his sane circumstantiis permitti poterit christianis, habito etiam respectu ad favorem fidei, ut possint eiusmodi captivos iusto pretio aut alio iusto titulo acquirere, et in propriam servitutem redigere et retinere, dummodo eo animo sint ut eos tractent secundum praecepta caritatis christianae, et curent etiam rudimentis fidei illos imbuere, adeo ut, si fieri poterit, in libertatem filiorum Dei, quae in sola catholica ecclesia est, nulla tamen coactione facta, sed tantummodo opportunis suasionibus et hortationibus, libere et feliciter traducantur per eorum conversionem ad veram fidem. Et hac de re prae oculis habeatur instructio s. m. Pii VI (12 Sept. 1776) quae adnectitur. (V. n. 515).

Quemadmodum vero servi licite emi, ita licite quoque vendi possunt, sed necessarium omnino est ut qui vendit legitimus sit servi possessor, nihilque in venditione committat quo servi alienandi vitae, honestati, aut catholicae fidei noceatur. Quare illicitum est

bought or received, since the captives themselves are masters of their own liberty, although it has been unjustly taken from them. If indeed, after they have been fully taught that freedom belongs to them by right and which they lose only by injury to others, they spontaneously and by their own free will, as masters of themselves, present themselves to Christians to be received by them and held in servitude, by a prudent plan in order to be freed from the harsh present servitude, from which they have in no way the ability to free themselves, and choose a milder servitude in the hands of Christian buyers and with whom they are easily able to persuade themselves that they can come to a knowledge of worshipping the true God, and of confessing Him to the inestimable advantage of their souls; in such circumstances it is permissible for the Christians, especially when they act in favor of the Faith, to purchase such captives for a just price, and to take and retain them in their own servitude, as long as they are of the mind to treat them according to the precepts of Christian charity, and take care to imbue them with the rudiments of the Faith so that, if it is possible, they may be freely and happily led, this being done by no compulsion, but only by oppor-

servum vendere, aut quomodocumque in proprietatem cedere alicui domino, qui certo aut probabili iudicio praevideatur servum eumdem inhumaniter habiturus vel ad peccatum pertracturus vel eodem abusurus ad iniquissimum illud commercium exercendum, quod Apostolicis Romanorum Pontificum, ac praesertim s. m. Gregorii XVI constitutionibus reprobatur districteque prohibetur. Illicitum pariter est servum alienare, nulla prorsus habita ratione iurium et officiorum matrimonialium ipsius servi. Multo magis illicitum est servum christianum vendere domino infideli, aut etiam, ubi perversionis periculum prudenter timendum sit, domino haeretico vel schismatico. Haec si Vicarius Ap. probe teneat, aperte videbit, quid respondendum sit ad 13, 14 et 15 dubium. Nihil enim impedit quominus familia christiana, de qua agitur in dubio 13, servos suos vendere tuta conscientia queat, si ipsos legitime possideat, et cautiones supra descriptas in venditione observet. Sic etiam negotiator in dubio 14 memoratus poterit ad sacramenta admitti, si constet, servos, qui ei pro mercium pretio obtigerunt, neque per furtum legitimo eorum domino subductos, neque iniuste in captivitatem redactos fuisse, ac

tune persuasion and encouragement, through their conversion to the True Faith into the liberty of the sons of God which is found only in the Catholic Church. On this matter one should look at the instruction of His Holiness Pius VI (Sept. 12, 1776), which is attached.

Indeed, just as slaves can be licitly bought, so they can licitly also be sold, but it is altogether necessary that the seller is the legitimate possessor of the slave, and does nothing in the sale by which the life, morals or Catholic faith of the slave to be sold would be harmed. Therefore it is illicit to sell a slave or in any manner give the slave into the ownership of any master who by a certain or probable judgment can be foreseen to be going to treat that slave inhumanely, or lead him to sin or abuse him for the sake of that most evil trade which has been condemned and strictly prohibited by the constitutions of the Roman Pontiffs, especially by Pope Gregory XVI. Likewise it is illicit to sell a slave, taking no account of the marriage rights and duties of that same slave. Much more illicit is it so sell a Christian slave to a faithless master, or even, where the danger of falling away is prudently to be feared, to an heretical or schismatic master. If he keeps these things properly

praeterea spondeat, se eos honestis conditionibus ita venditurum esse, ut nihil ex eiusmodi venditione laedantur vel periclitentur iura et officia, quae illis tamquam hominibus, et, si christianam fidem amplexi fuerint, tamquam fidelibus competunt. Tandem de dubio 15 statuendum est christianos ipsos, etiam missionarios, interesse posse ut testes et sequestres aliove nomine per sacros canones non prohibito, contractibus, indiciis, aliisque id genus publicis actibus servorum causa fieri solitis, qui tamen et in se liciti sint, et nulla prava circumstantia vitientur.

V. Sequitur quarta dubiorum classis, de servis fugitivis. Mancipium iuxta leges Gallarum et Sidamarum in rerum utilium numero censetur, de quibus verum propriumque dominium habetur, et fiunt contractus, quaeque deperditae conquiruntur, raptae aut usurpatae apud iudices repetuntur. Hinc quaeritur:

"16. An liceat christianis ipsisque missionariis servos suos fugitivos persequi, atque ad redeundum cogere, vel saltem permittere ut eosdem persequantur, et vi etiam adhibita reducant publicus magistratus aut amici.

"17. An servi ius habeant ad fugam, et an debeant resarcire

in mind, the Vicar Apostolic will clearly see what response is to be given to questions 13, 14, and 15. For nothing impedes any Christian family — as mentioned in question 13 — from selling their slaves in good conscience, if they possess them legitimately and, in the sale, observe the cautions described above. So also the seller mentioned in question 14 can be admitted to the sacraments if it is a fact that the slaves who have come into his possession as pay, have not been taken from their rightful master by theft nor been unjustly reduced to slavery, and if he furthermore solemnly promises that he will sell them in such moral conditions that none of the rights and duties which belong to them as men — and, if they have embraced the Christian faith, as Christians — will be harmed or endangered by the sale. Finally in respect to question 15 it is determined that the Christians themselves, even missionaries, can be present as witnesses and as agents — or any other name not prohibited by the sacred canons — in contracts, judgments and other public acts of this types done in respect to slaves as long as the acts are licit in themselves and are vitiated by no evil circumstance.

V. Next we come to the

damna ex eorum fuga domino illata."

"18 ...

"19 ...

Quemadmodum adnotatum est in responsione ad postulata proxime superiora, sunt iusti aliqui tituli seu causae, ex quibus potest servus libertate sua legitime privari, legitimeque a domino retineri. Porro cum manifeste repugnet, hinc quidem ius domino competere possidendi ac retinendi servum, inde autem ius servo inesse ne a domino possideatur ac retineatur, nemo non videt christianos et missionarios de quibus agitur in dubio 16, posse tuta conscientia servos suos fugitivos persequi, et ad redeundum cogere, siquidem eos iuste in servitutem redactos iusto ex titulo possideant.

Non ita expedita est ad 17 et 18 dubium responsio. Regulariter fugere iure suo possunt servi qui iniuste fuerint in servitutem redacti; non possunt servi qui iustam subeant servitutem, nisi forte a domino sollicitentur ad ali quod peccatum, vel inhumaniter tractentur. Ex hac distinctione pendet solutio alterius quaestionis, an scilicet servi fugitivi teneantur resarcire damna ex fuga sua domino illata. Cum enim ad inducendam restituendi damni obligationem tria haec simul et coniunctim requirantur,

questions about fugitive slaves. According to the laws of the Galla and Sidama the slave is counted among the useful things over which one has a true and proper dominion, and for which they make contracts, damages are sought, and judgment sought in case of theft or usurpation. Hence it is asked:

"16. Whether it is licit for Christians and for missionaries themselves to search for fugitive slaves, and force them to return, or at least to permit that others search them out or even by use of force have the public magistrate or friends bring them back.

"17. Whether slaves have the right to flight, and whether they have to repair the damages caused by their flight to the master.

"18 ...

"19 ...

As has been noted in response to the questions immediately above, there are some just titles or causes by which a slave can be legitimately deprived of his liberty and legitimately retained by a master. But since it is contradictory to say that a master has the right to possess and retain a slave and the slave has the right not to be possessed and retained by a master, everyone can see that the Christians and missionaries mentioned in question 16 are able in good conscience to search for

culpa theologica, damnum secutum, et causa efficax, patet profecto ad reficienda damna ex fuga sua domino illata, tenere servos illos quorum fuga fuit graviter illicita, non teneri servos illos quorum fuga omni caruit culpa; sed de liceitate fugae, deque obligatione resarciendi damna ex fuga illata consulat Vic. Ap. probatos auctores et cum illis distinguat varios casus, variosque servitutis titulos.

fugitive slaves and force them to return, if indeed they possess a just title to those who have been justly reduced to slavery.

It is not so easy to answer questions 17 and 18. Regularly it is the right of slaves who have been unjustly reduced to slavery to flee; it is not permitted for slaves who undergo just servitude, unless perhaps they are solicited by the master to some sin, or are treated inhumanly. On this distinction depends the solution to the other question, namely whether fugitive slaves are held to make up for the damage caused to the master by their flight. Since, to incur the obligation of restitution three conditions must be simultaneously linked together and fulfilled, viz. theological sin, subsequent damage, and efficacious cause, it is clear that those slaves whose flight was gravely illicit are held to reparation while those slaves whose flight lacked all fault are not; but as to the liceity of flight and the obligation of repairing the damage caused by such flight let the Vicar Apostolic consult the approved authors and with them distinguish between the various cases and the various titles to servitude.

APPENDIX D

Pope John Paul II

Here is what the Holy Father had to say on the occasion of his visit to the church of St. Charles Borromeo on the Island of Gorée, Saturday, February 22, 1992:

Dear Brothers and Sisters,

    1. With all my heart I greet you.

Let me tell you of my joy and emotion upon paying a visit to this famous island of Gorée, whose history and the architectural quality of its ancient dwellings have made it part of mankind's world patrimony.

Yet, at the same time as my joy, I would like to share with you my profound emotion, the emotion that one naturally experiences in a place like this, so profoundly marked by the inconsistencies of the human heart, the scene of an eternal struggle between light and darkness, between good and evil, between grace and sin. Gorée, the symbol of the coming of the Gospel of freedom, is also, unfortunately, the symbol of the appalling madness of those who reduced into slavery their brothers and sisters to whom the Gospel of freedom was destined.

The Pope, who deeply experiences the joys and hopes as well as the sorrows and anguish of people, cannot be insensitive to all that Gorée represents.

    2. In coming here, dear brothers and sisters, it is first of all a pilgrimage to the sources of the Catholic Church in Senegal that I am making. Indeed, in the 15th century Gorée welcomed the first Catholic priests, the chaplains of the Portuguese caravels which called here. Certainly the Good News of salvation in Jesus Christ did not immediately spread throughout the continent, but later Gorée and Saint-Louis became veritable centers of evangelization; the Pope is happy to pay homage to their influence. Besides Gorée has the honor of having given the Church the

first Senegalese priests of modern times, and it is from Gorée that in 1846 the missionaries of Venerable Father Libermann went to found the mission in Dakar.

In this church dedicated to Charles Borromeo, a saint who is personally dear to me, it is good to recall and become more aware of the great grace which the coming of God's kingdom represents for this part of the world. We rejoice that, in the measure of the hidden plan of divine Providence, the Lord's prayer has been granted, the prayer which we have just heard and which the Church ceaselessly repeats throughout the ages: "Our Father in heaven, hallowed be your name, your kingdom come!" (Mt 6:10). Yes, we thank God for having sent his apostles here and, repeating the words of the psalmist, we praise him because "through all the earth their voice resounds, and to the ends of the world their message" (Ps 19[18]:5).

When he entrusted to his disciples what he called "his" commandment, "Love one another as I have loved you" Christ added these words: "No one has greater love than this, to lay down one's life for one's friends" (Jn 15:13). He announced what he was going to accomplish by his death on the cross, by his blood poured out for us and for all people. The Apostles and martyrs, united to the Savior's passion, imitated him in this witness, as did the saints of all ages who knew how to offer the gift of their life for the sake of the kingdom of God. It is to this glorious line of heralds of the Gospel that the pioneers of faith belong, those who came to this country to sow the seed of the word of God and offer their life for their African friends. I am happy to give thanks with you for all that has been achieved by the generations of missionaries: priests and catechists; men and women religious; of this last group there is the beautiful figure of Anne-Marie Javouhey who, with so many others, gave a remarkable example of true love of God and neighbor. These Gospel workers formed solid local structures which enabled it to take root. Today the Catholic Church has her place in Senegal, a modest position, but a real one; and she is witnessing a new evangelical energy, as is shown especially by your archdiocesan synod to which you, as the Catholic community of the island of Gorée, are contributing.

Thinking of the heritage of the past and what has followed it in the present, with all my heart I say, with the zealous missionary, St. Paul: "Thanks be to God for this indescribable gift!" (2 Cor 9:15).

3. However, in coming to Gorée, where we would like to be able to devote ourselves entirely to the joy of thanksgiving, how can we not be overcome by sadness at the thought of the other facts which this place

stirs up? The visit to the "slave house" recalls to mind that enslavement of black people which in 1462 Pius II, writing to a missionary Bishop who was leaving for Guinea, described as the "enormous crime," the "*magnum scelus.*" Throughout a whole period of the history of the African continent, black men, women and children were brought to this cramped space, uprooted from their land and separated from their loved ones to be sold as goods. They came from all different countries and, parting in chains for new lands, they retained as the last image of their native Africa Gorée's basalt rock cliffs. We could say that this island is fixed in the memory and heart of all the black diaspora.

These men, women and children were the victims of a disgraceful trade in which people who were baptized, but who did not live their faith, took part. How can we forget the enormous suffering inflicted, the violation of the most basic human rights, on those people deported from the African continent? How can we forget the human lives destroyed by slavery?

In all truth and humility this sin of man against man, this sin of man against God, must be confessed. How far the human family still has to go until its members learn to look at and respect one another as God's image, in order to love one another as sons and daughters of their common heavenly Father!

From this African shrine of black sorrow, we implore heaven's forgiveness. We pray that in the future Christ's disciples will be totally faithful to the observance of the commandment of fraternal love which the Master left us. We pray that never again will people oppress their brothers and sisters, whoever they may be, but always seek to imitate the compassion of the Good Samaritan in the Gospel in going to help those who are in need. We pray that the scourge of slavery and all its effects may disappear forever: do not recent tragic incidents on this continent too invite us to be watchful and continue this lengthy, laborious process of conversion of heart? We must equally oppose the new, often insidious forms of slavery, such as organized prostitution which shamefully takes advantage of the poverty of the people of the Third World.

In this era of crucial changes, today's Africa suffers severely from the draining of its living forces which has been going on for some time. In certain regions its human resources have been weakened for a long time. The aid which Africa has a pressing need of is also its just due. May God grant that an active solidarity be exercised in its behalf so that it may overcome these tragic difficulties!

4. To conclude this meeting, at the end of our universal prayer, we will invoke Mary, Mother of mercy. In our deep sorrow for the sins of the past, especially for those that this place reminds us of, let us ask her to be "our advocate" to her Son. Let us pray to her that violence and injustice between people will come to an end that no new pits of hatred and vengeance will be dug, but that respect, harmony and friendship among all peoples may grow.

At a time when in Africa, Europe, America and all the regions of the world the proclamation of the Good News of Christ must gain new energy through generous initiatives, let us offer our prayer that the kingdom of her Son may come, that "kingdom of life and truth, the kingdom of grace and holiness, that kingdom of justice, love and peace" (cf. Preface for the Feast of Christ, King of the Universe).

Select Bibliography

Acta Leonis XIII.

Acta Sanctae Sedis.

Attwater, Donald. *The White Fathers in Africa*. London: Burns Oates and Washbourne, Ltd., 1937.

Baronius. *Annales Ecclesiastici*, Vol. 28. Edited by O. Raynaldus. Luca: 1752.

Brandi, Salvatore M., S.J. *Il Papato e la Schiavitù*. Rome: Civiltà Cattolica, 1903.

_____. "Il Papato e la Schiavitù." *La Civiltà Cattolica* X (1903): 545-61, 677-94.

Bullarium Benedicti XIV, Tome I. Rome: 1746.

Carlen, Claudia, editor. *The Papal Encyclicals, 1878-1903*. Raleigh: McGrath, 1981.

Coleccion de documentos ineditos relativos al descubrimiento, conquista y organizacion de las antiguas posesiones espanolas de America y Oceania, sacados de los archivos del reino y muy especialmente del de Indias. Madrid: 1864-84. Vol. 12.

Collectanea S. Congregationis de Propaganda Fide seu Decreta, Instructiones, Rescripta pro Apostolicis Missionibus, Vol. I. Rome: Polyglot Press, 1907.

Denzinger-Huenermann. *Enchiridion Symbolorum*. Rome: Herder, 1991.

Dussel, Enrique, ed. *The Church in Latin America: 1492-1992*. Maryknoll, NY: Orbis Books, 1992.

Ellis, John Tracy. *Documents of American Catholic History*, Vol. I. Wilmington, Delaware: Michael Glazier, Inc., 1987.

Eppstein, John. *The Catholic Tradition of the Law of the Nations*. London: Burns, Oates and Washbourne, Ltd., 1935.

Gannon, Michael V. *Rebel Bishop: The Life and Era of Augustin Verot*. Milwaukee: Bruce Publishing Company, 1964.

Gutierrez, Gustavo. *Las Casas: In Search of the Poor of Jesus Christ*. Maryknoll, NY: Orbis Books, 1993.

Hanke, Lewis. "Pope Paul III and the American Indians." *Harvard Theological Review* XXX (April 1937): 69-101.

Hennesey, James, S.J. *American Catholics: A History of the Roman Catholic Community in the United States.* New York: Oxford University Press, 1981.

Hernaez, Francisco Javier, S.J., ed. *Coleccion de Bulas, Breves y Otros Documentos Relativos a la Iglesia de America y Filipinas,* Vols. I and II. Brussels: Imprenta de Alfredo, 1879.

Kelly, J.N.D. *The Oxford Dictionary of the Popes.* Oxford: Oxford University Press, 1986.

Kenrick, Francis Patrick. *Theologia Moralis,* I. Philadelphia: 1841.

Las Casas, Bartolome de. *The Only Way.* Edited by Helen Rand Parish, translated by Francis P. Sullivan. Mahwah, N.J.: Paulist Press, 1992.

MacNutt, Francis. *Bartholomew De Las Casas: His Life, His Apostolate, and His Writings.* New York: G.P. Putnam's Sons, 1909.

Maxwell, John F. *Slavery and the Catholic Church.* Chichester: Ross, 1975.

New Catholic Encyclopedia, The. Washington: Catholic University of America, 1967. S.v. "Slavery (History of)," by C. Verlinden.

New Encyclopedia Britannica, The. Chicago: Encyclopedia Britannica, Inc., 1985. S.v. "Vitoria, Francisco de," by B.M.H.

Noonan, John T. Jr. "Development in Moral Doctrine." *Theological Studies* 54 (December 1993): 662-77.

Panzer, Joel S. "Slavery: A Change in Church Teaching?" *Dunwoodie Review* 17 (1994): 129-35.

Parish, Helen Rand and Harold E. Weidman. *Las Casas en Mexico: Historia y obras desconocidas.* Mexico: Fondo de Cultura Economica, 1992.

Pastor, Ludwig. *The History of the Popes,* XII. Edited by Ralph Francis Kerr. St. Louis: Herder, 1912.

Reynolds, Ignatius Aloysius, editor. *The Works of the Right Rev. John England, III.* Baltimore: John Murphy & Co., 1849.

"Santa Sede e L'Inghilterra Nell'Anno 1814, La." *Civiltà Cattolica* VII (1902): 157-79.

Thomas, Hugh. *Conquest: Montezuma, Cortes, and the Fall of Old Mexico.* New York: Simon and Schuster, 1993.

INDEX

A

Alexander III, 60
Alexander VI, 11-14
Altitudo Divini Consilii, 24, 66
Attwater, Donald, 61

B

Baltimore, 1840 Council of, 68
Benedict XIV, 38-43, 45, 60, 65, 66
Bishops (American), failure to condemn slavery, 48, 55
Brandi, Salvatore, 27-28, 28-29f, 43f

C

Cambodia, 54
Canary Islands, 7-11
Catholicae Ecclesiae, 58-61
Centesimus Annus, 10
Charles V, 22, 23-34
Church teaching, dissent from, 10, 48, 55, 68-71
Clement I, 45
Clergy, and slavery, 12, 41-42, 44-45, 46, 66, 68, 69, 70
Columbus, Christopher, 12
Commissum Nobis, 31-34, 40, 89-91
Consalvi, Cardinal, 43-44f
Cum Sicuti, 29-31, 86-88

D

Death penalty, 3-4
De Lugo, Cardinal Juan, 27f
De Unico Modo (The Only Way), 17f, 25f
Diartano, Francisco, 32
Doctrine of the Faith, Congregation for, 35
Dom Pedro II, Emperor, 58

E

Ellis, John Tracy, 19f, 23f
England, John, 48, 67-69
Eppstein, John, 18f, 26
Eugene IV, 7 10, 41
Evangelium Vitae, 4
Excommunication, penalty of, 9-10, 22, 23-24, 24f, 25, 34, 39, 41, 42f, 65

Eximiae Devotionis, 11, 13f

F

Faith:
  able to be received by all, 14, 15, 18-19, 20, 21, 22-23, 24, 26, 58-59, 64, 65
  excuse for enslavement, 15, 16, 19-20, 29-30, 35
Ferdinand, King (and Queen Isabella), 11-12
Forsyth, John (Secretary of State), 48, 68

G

Gannon, Michael, 67
Gaudium et Spes, 2
Geneva Conventions, 3
Gregory the Great, 60
Gregory IX, 60
Gregory XVI, 29-31, 44-48, 54-55, 60, 65, 67-69
Gutierrez, Gustavo, 14f, 16, 21f, 23f, 65-66

H

Hadrian I, 60
Hanke, Lewis, 23f, 65
Hennesey, James, 47, 48, 67
Hernaez, 13f, 14, 32f
Holy Office Response No. 230, 34-38, 103-104
Holy Office Response No. 515, 54, 105-106
Holy Office Response No. 1293, 48-56, 107-115
Hurbon, Laennec, 2, 47

I

Immensa Pastorum, 38-43, 92-96
Ineffabilis et Summi Patris, 13-14
Innocent III, 60
Innocent XI, 34-38
In Plurimis, 56-58, 60
In Supremo, 44-48, 67-69, 97-102
Inter Caetera, 11-13, 12f, 13 f, 21

J

Jansen, Cornelius, 32
John Paul II, 4, 10, 117-119, 123

K

Kelly, J.N.D., 48
Kenrick, Archbishop Francis Patrick, 69
King, Martin Luther, Jr., vii-viii

L

Las Casas, Bartolome de, 12f, 14f, 15, 16, 17f, 25, 25f, 70
Lavigerie, Cardinal Charles, 60-61, 70
Leo X, 60
Leo XIII, 56-61, 59f, 65

M

Manning, Cardinal Henry, 61
Massaia, Rev. William, 49
Maxwell, John F., 2, 5f, 7f, 12f, 13f, 18f, 22f, 27f, 32f, 38f, 48, 59f, 63, 65
Mission, The (movie), 1
Motu Proprio, 1548, 27-28

N

Non Indecens Videtus, 23, 43f, 66
Noonan, John T., 2, 27f, 47, 51 f, 56f, 63

P

Parish, Helen Rand, 16-18, 25
Pastorale Officium, 18, 19, 22-24, 33, 40, 41, 43f, 65, 66, 84-85
Paul III, 16-28, 40-41, 45, 60, 64, 65, 66
Philip II, 30, 31
Philip IV, 32
Pius II, 10, 45, 60, 119
Pius V, 29f
Pius VI, 54
Pius VII, 43, 43f, 45, 60
Pius IX, 48-56, 49f
Portugal, 1-2, 11-14

Propagation of the Faith, Congregation for, 61

R

Rerum Novarum, 10
Restitution, 30,31

S

Servitude, indentured, 52
Servitude, just-title, 35, 36-38, 50-55, 56, 64
Servitude, symbiotic, 52, 54
Sixtus IV, 10
Slavery:
  and the condemnation of the slave trade, 46-48, 67-69
  consistency of papal teaching against, 69-70
  in the culture of tribal peoples, 15f, 26, 26f, 49-50, 56
  previously unheard of, 4, 19-20
  racial, 5, 35-38, 63-64
  right to flee from, 55
  subtle forms of today, 70-71, 119
Spain, 1-2, 11-14
Sicut Dudum, 7-10, 41, 75-78
Sublimis Deus, 4, 16-21, 25-26, 33, 64, 65, 66, 79-81

T

Tavera, Cardinal Juande, 22
Thomas, Hugh, 15f, 20, 26f
Tordessillas, Treaty of, 12-13

U

Urban VIII, 31-34, 40-41, 45, 60, 65

V

Van Buren, President Martin, 48, 68
Veritas Ipsa, 17, 82-83
Vienna, Congress of, 43, 43-44f
Vitoria, Francisco de, 4, 25-27, 27f

W

White Fathers, 60-61

Cover Photo

THE SLAVE HOUSE on the Island of Gorée was built about 1780 and is typical of the houses of the slave traders. The ground floor contains the dark, damp cells where the slaves were kept while awaiting transit; the upper floor was the home of the slave trader, his family, domestic staff and craftsmen. The male slaves were chained at all times while women and children were unchained at night. More than chains, however, prevented the slaves from escaping. The island's geography and the sharks in the surrounding waters were also an effective deterrent. An estimated 60,000 of the 12,000,000 Africans taken as slaves sailed from Gorée. The "slave house" has been restored by the Senegalese government with international aid; today it serves as a museum and is registered by UNESCO as part of mankind's universal cultural heritage.

After his visit to the slave house on Gorée, Pope John Paul II expressed his thoughts in a few extemporaneous remarks in French, which are given here in English translation.

"It is a cry! ... I have come here to listen to the cry of the centuries and generations, the generations of Blacks, of slaves. Now, at the same time, I am thinking that Jesus Christ came, one might say, as a slave, a servant: but he brought light even into this situation of slavery. This light was called the presence of God, liberation in God... liberation in God, that is, the God who is Love.

"Here one thinks first and foremost about injustice: it is a tragedy of the civilization which claimed to be Christian. The great philosopher of antiquity, Socrates, said that those who find themselves in a situation of injustice are in a better condition than those who cause injustice.

"However, it is the other side of the reality of injustice which took place here. There is a human drama. This cry of the centuries, of generations, demands we free ourselves ever more from this drama because the roots of this tragedy are in us, in human nature, in sin.

"I have come here to pay homage to all these victims, unknown victims; no one knows exactly how many there were; no one knows exactly who they were. Unfortunately, our civilization which called itself Christian, which claims to be Christian, returned to this situation of anonymous slaves in our century; we know what concentration camps were: here is a model for them. One can not plumb the depths of the tragedy of our civilization, of our weakness, of sin. We must remain ever faithful to a different appeal, that of Saint Paul who said, 'Ubi abundavit peccatum superabundavit gratia.' Where sin abounded, grace abounded even more: grace, that means love, abounded even more."